Lord, have You forgotten me?

JUDITH COUCHMAN

WORD PUBLISHING
Dallas · London · Vancouver · Melbourne

LORD, HAVE YOU FORGOTTEN ME?

Library of Congress Cataloging-in-Publication Data:

Couchman, Judith, 1953–
   Lord, have you forgotten me? / Judith Couchman.
      p. cm.
   Includes bibliographical references.
   ISBN 0-8499-5010-4
   1. Women—Religious life. 2. Self-realization—Religious aspects—Christianity. I. Title.
   BV4527.C68 1992
   242'.643—dc20   92–24377
                                                                      CIP

Printed in the United States of America
2 3 4 5 9 LB 9 8 7 6 5 4 3 2 1

In memory of my father,
Harold Wayne Couchman

ALSO BY JUDITH COUCHMAN

Getting a Grip on Guilt
If I'm So Good, Why Don't I Act That Way?
Lord, Please Help Me to Change
Why Is Her Life Better Than Mine?

Contents

Acknowledgments

*A*lthough I didn't know my father very well because of his early death, I feel he's largely responsible for this book. Through him, I inherited the German perseverance—the downright stubbornness—it takes to solicit and write a manuscript for publication.

Old newspaper obituaries describe my grandfather and great-grandfather Couchman as hardworking farmers; my dad worked hard, too. By example, he taught me not to give up when life gets me down. And that is the collective message of these devotional readings.

At Word Publishing, I'm grateful to Carol Bartley, a patient and insightful editor who taught me much about southern graciousness, and to Dan Rich, mentor and friend, who once again believed in my abilities. And in Colorado Springs, I'm thankful for Claudia Stafford, who offered uncomplaining help with typing and chasing details, and Deena Davis, who sensitively copyedited the manuscript.

Thanks also to those who prayed: Charette Barta, Opal Couchman, Madalene Harris, Karen Hilt, Shirley Honeywell, Mae Lammers and Nancy Lemons.

THIS IS YOUR LIFE

And it's not what you wanted

bsolutely, it's a day I'll never forget. It was the day my high school choir director tacked up a list of lead roles for the spring musical. The day my name wasn't on the list. The day the real world crashed my dream to act on stage.

This can't be true, I thought, as I choked inside and scanned the list again with teary eyes. I was supposed to be the lead! But I wasn't. I wasn't even an understudy.

I held some reason to believe I'd capture the lead role. As a junior, I'd been the only underclassman to play a secondary lead in the musical, and often that person landed the plum role in his or her senior year.

Falling short of that expectation felt humiliating. But to make it worse, the choir director, perhaps in a moment of guilt or insanity, listed me with the *dancers* for the musical.

Me? Clumsy, overweight, never-had-a-dance-lesson-in-my-life me? I hadn't even tried out for a dance role! And for the next few months of rehearsals, I proved that I could not, *would not* choose a career for which I needed full-body coordination.

Looking back twenty years later, I realize why the choreographer kept me in the back row of dancers. (I remember tromping on my partner's feet a few times.) And I can laugh . . . a little.

It's not that I still feel the pain; it's that I remember how this episode hurtled me into the real world. A world riddled with disappointments. A world in which dreams, prayers, and preparation don't always award me with the part I want to play.

I don't like the real world. It's full of computers that crash, plans that fall apart, and friends who don't understand me. It holds no guarantees against layoffs from work, children who die, or husbands who leave wives. In other words, the real world doesn't fit the formula that says, "If you really believe in something, or if you act the 'right' way, then life will fulfill your desires."

And in the real world, I struggle against the feeling that, in certain areas of my life, God has forgotten me.

Do you struggle with that feeling, too?

It's not uncommon. Whether we acknowledge it or not, we all pass through times when life doesn't make sense to us. We do, we dream, we hope, we pray—and still God doesn't fulfill our desires.

Why does He keep us waiting? Or why does He sometimes say no? I don't presume to know. But through the years and with hindsight, I'm growing to trust His magnificent wisdom in waiting to change circumstances. And to understand that the greatest miracle is how He changes me while I'm waiting.

But right now, that probably doesn't help you. You need hope, encouragement, and the reassurance that God loves you and listens to your pleas. You long for comfort when your name isn't on the list. You need courage to dance gracefully when you don't recognize the step. You want to know that God hasn't forgotten you or your requests.

And that's the underlying intent of this book: to gird your unsettled soul; to console you while you wait; to help you live with unfulfilled desires. Yet, if these readings only offered encouragement, they'd hurt more than help you. You also need exhortation—words that rattle your thinking and kick where you need it—because sometimes we place the total responsibility on God and ignore our part in fulfilling personal desires. And there's plenty we can do to actively participate in the waiting process.

So if life isn't what you want it to be, these thirty readings of stories and Scriptures can help you live a meaningful life, despite unfulfilled dreams, and grasp God's hope for the future. You'll also examine your attitudes and expectations—and how they could hinder your progress toward contented living.

Five sections will help you explore . . .

- the ways unrealistic expectations grow.
- barriers to obtaining unfulfilled desires.
- sinful actions and attitudes that can develop.
- how to accept life, one day at a time.
- what it takes to wait for God's answer.

Still, these readings won't tell you how to convince God to deliver what you want. Instead, they'll encourage you to keep trusting Him—and to live for today while waiting for tomorrow. Because you don't know what tomorrow may bring.

For me, "tomorrow" unfolded God's plan, and I wound up better because of it. For the long haul, I didn't possess enough talent to pursue an acting or singing career. These were a high school girl's fantasies. Ironically, the rejection edged me into studying journalism, and that's how I support myself today. My talent and personality fit this career, and working as a writer turned my life into an adventure—and that's what I'd wanted all along.

On the other hand, I still live with unfulfilled expectations in other areas of life. And in telling this high school story, I don't mean to trivialize the agony of waiting for a husband, a baby who's difficult to conceive, a job that doesn't feel like torture, a recovery from long-term illness, or a return to "normal" life after a loved one's death.

Rather, it's to say that whatever the size of your unfulfilled expectations, God has not forgotten you. No matter is too small or too big for Him. He turns losses into gains. And however He answers your prayers, He's always interested in being the God whom you'll never forget.

—*Judith Couchman*

Note: In some of the following readings, the author altered names and circumstances to protect identities.

Part One

TALL TALES

Living in a world of high expectations

e want life to be a neat package tied with a pretty bow. Everything must make sense, all the transitions obvious. We like our people that way, too. We would prefer everyone to be predictable characters in a potboiler—the villain, the innocent beauty, the hero. Because we don't like loose ends, unresolved issues, unexplained events, or contrary families, we beg God to let us write the story—or at least read ahead. Just once, we'd like to skip from chapter three to chapter eleven. But that's not the kind of reading God wants us to do. We've got to take the plot as it unfolds, with all its unexpected and unexplained twists and turns. God wants us to make the connections between the seemingly unconnected events and people in our lives.[1]

Cheryl Forbes,
Catching Sight of God

I once worked with a man who, every summer, retreated to the woods to fight with his wife. It's not that he planned to argue with his spouse. The couple actually embarked on an annual camping trip to relax in the forest. But without fail, a few days into their vacation the conflict began.

For this couple, getting away from responsibility focused their attention on each other—and the grievances they harbored. So each year, with nature as their witness, they verbally duked out the pain, anger, and disappointment in their marriage.

"Actually, I think those annual fights hold our marriage together," he chuckled as he told me. "They give us a chance to air our dirty laundry. We probably wouldn't survive if we didn't do that now and then."

Fortunately, my colleague and his wife possessed a good sense of humor. Without it, their marriage would have fallen prey to a menace that kills countless marital and other relationships: the pain of unmet expectations. Often these expectations revolve around people: friends, bosses, partners, children, work associates, family members, people in authority. We build expectations toward them; they create expectations toward us.

But we also build expectations toward the "things" in our lives: work, cars, houses, clothing, education, even entertainment. And if these expectations don't affect relationships, they can at least clobber us personally when they fail to please us.

Then, of course, there's the unrelenting expectations we create for our personal selves: a hard body, a peaceful spirit, a beautiful face, an intelligent mind, a witty sense of humor. Who can measure up to all of these?

That's not to say all expectations are bad. To expect nothing from life or people robs us of hope and vibrancy, even normalcy. We expect to spend time with family; we expect to learn from the night class we're attending; we expect to find a decent-paying job; we expect our children to return home after school. But when we create rigid or unrealistic expectations and clutch them, there's no joy or contentment, either. We live in a broken world, so people and plans and things will eventually fail us, no matter how hard we try.

Unfortunately, at this point, it's easy to blame God for our unmet expectations. We ask, "God, why did You ignore me?"

when maybe we should ask, "Lord, were my expectations unrealistic? Were they built on my fantasies instead of Your truths?" Sometimes we rail at God for our own messes—for plans He didn't create and things He didn't intend for us.

So what's the key to living with expectations? It's holding them with both hope and reality, yet anchoring them in God's ways instead of our ideas.

"Your ways are not like my ways," says the Lord (Isaiah 55:8b). But when we follow His ways, that's when living really begins!

PERSONAL CHECKPOINT

In Part One, consider how unrealistic expectations develop, how they lead to dashed dreams, and how you can develop expectations built on God's Kingdom values.

1. What unmet expectations do you struggle with?

2. In what ways are these expectations realistic? In what ways are they unrealistic?

3. How can you know you're hanging on to the right expectations, with both hope and realism?

Stories Mother Told You

Childhood promises don't always come true, but we can depend on the surety of God's Word.

I am a woman in conflict," announced my thirtysomething friend as she entered the room wearing an oversized Minnie Mouse shirt and carrying a Dooney & Bourke briefcase.

She had just returned from a business trip to Anaheim, California, where she had also visited Disneyland. That morning, it was tough re-entering the real world of meetings and expectations, so she arrived wearing a tribute to childhood dreams while holding in her hand a symbol of adult responsibilities. (Luckily, we're not a business-suit type of group.)

"I just wanted the fantasy to last a bit longer," she laughed and explained. We nodded knowingly. Disney does that to people.

Later, after the others left, my friend confided, "You know, there's a whole lot more to this fantasy thing than I admit to most people. When I'm at Disneyland, I find myself wanting to buy all of the stuffed characters, scoop up the videos of old movies, and ride every attraction related to fairy tales of my girlhood. And whenever I walk through Sleeping Beauty's castle and hear, 'When you wish upon a star,' I start to cry."

She choked back tears and explained, "That song reminds me that my childhood dreams haven't come true."

*A*s young girls, our mothers probably read stories to us. We remember those treasured moments, filled with foibles and morals, dangers and dilemmas, courageous characters and happy endings. With drowsy eyes, we could imagine most anything and believe that dreams come true.

As we grew older and could better distinguish between "real" and "pretend," Mom discarded the Brothers Grimm and Mother Goose to weave her own tales. In these stories her children emerged as the main characters in plots that comforted and protected us:

"One day, you'll marry a perfect man."

"You'll have beautiful children someday."

"I know your life will be happier than mine."

We believed these stories. Or at least we wanted to. They represented Mom's best hopes for us, her endless confidence in us, her vision of who we could be. And with these stories, she wished us no harm.

Along the way to adulthood, we collected other stories, too: from Dad, friends, teachers, siblings, preachers, movies, television, advertising. It seemed everyone told us stories about who we should be, what we should do, how we should think. But instead of clarifying our vision, the stories piled so high they blurred our view of reality. We began to think that everything we wanted in life would materialize before us. Until one day, something failed to appear and we smashed into the unbending truth: the promises of youth don't always come true.

*W*hen we discover that childhood stories don't come true, it can feel slightly annoying or, as with my colleague, deeply painful. Those promises built our expectations for an ideal world, with ourselves as the center of attention. It's startling to discover other players in the story who don't care about us.

This realization brings us to a crucial juncture that affects our emotional outlook. Clinging to childhood expectations can thread unhappiness throughout our lives. Dismantling these expectations and accepting reality can grow us toward maturity.

Still, maturity doesn't mean giving up hopes and dreams. It means our expectations stay rooted in daily reality and in the promises we can depend on. We find those promises in God's Word:

"Life will be tough, but I will never leave you."

"Your sins are forgiven and cast away forever."

"I'm preparing a lovely place for you in heaven."

When we shift our expectations toward the surety of the Scriptures, we discover that a King descended to earth for us. Although He won't banish the earthly trials of today, He'll accompany us toward the heavenly promises of tomorrow. And that's a story we can depend on.

Personal Checkpoint

1. What childhood dreams didn't come true for you?

2. How have childhood stories affected your adult expectations?

God's Viewpoint

Paul reminds Timothy:

Be strong in the grace we have in Christ Jesus. You should teach people whom you can trust the things you and many others have heard me say. Then they will be able to teach others. Share in the troubles we have like a good soldier of Christ Jesus.

Think about what I am saying, because the Lord will give you the ability to understand everything.

But you have followed what I teach, the way I live, my goal, faith, patience, and love. You know I never give up. You know how I have been hurt and have suffered, as in Antioch, Iconium, and Lystra. I have suffered, but the Lord saved me from all those troubles. Everyone who wants to live as God desires, in Christ Jesus, will be hurt. But people who are evil and cheat others will go from bad to worse. They will fool others, but they will also be fooling themselves.

But you should continue following the teachings you learned. You know they are true, because you trust those who taught you. Since you were a child you have known the Holy Scriptures which are able to make you wise. And that wisdom leads to salvation through faith in Christ Jesus. All Scripture is given by God and is useful for teaching, for showing people what is wrong in their lives, for correcting faults, and for teaching how to live right. Using the Scriptures, the person who serves God will be capable, having all that is needed to do every good work.

—2 Timothy 2:1-3, 7; 3:10-17

YOUR RESPONSE

1. How can the Scriptures help you develop realistic expectations? How can they help you still dream dreams?

2. What marks the difference between believing in fantasies and having faith in God's Word?

THE SEARCH FOR SUPERWOMAN

Society expects us to succeed at everything. God only asks us to fulfill His plan for us.

everal Februarys ago, a friend from Chicago visited me for what I thought would be some serious fun together. Before Nancy arrived, I mentally planned our activities: cooking, shopping, eating out, sightseeing, attending movies and theater, driving through the mountains, and talking, talking, talking.

Nancy has been my friend for many years, and through our twenties and thirties, we grabbed at life with the "you can have it all" motto pounding in our heads. During our times together, we often analyzed and strategized our potential: what we'd done, what we were doing, what we still wanted to do. We thrived on the possibilities ahead of us, and our to-do lists swelled to the capacity of Superwoman.

So I expected more of the same when Nancy landed in Colorado Springs to spend several days together.

The first full day of her visit, I worked at the office and Nancy stayed at home to regroup and relax. I knew her life had been busy, moving from an apartment into a fixer-upper house, teaching piano students, performing at concerts, and hostessing who-knows-what. But opening the door to my condo late that afternoon, I still anticipated her bounding toward me, maybe with some gourmet goodie she'd baked, exuding her usual charm.

Instead, silence greeted me.

"Nancy?" I queried, looking toward the stairway.

A sob floated down.

"Nancy?"

She appeared at the landing, still garbed in robe and slippers, with tissues clutched in her hands. Her red eyes suggested it hadn't been a good day.

"I'm sorry," she said. "I've been crying all day. Life is too much for me right now. I just need to fall apart."

So, as expected, we talked. But this time, about how something inside her had misfired. She needed a break from the stress; she wanted to switch off the schedule. Life at high speed was burning her up. There wasn't any more she could give. I nodded in agreement, thinking of the weariness I'd stuffed inside of me, hoping no one had noticed, and wondering, *Am I really supposed to be doing all of this?*

That's when we realized that, in our frantic search for Superwoman, we'd lost sight of ourselves.

*S*ince then, we've struggled toward changing our "I must do everything" lifestyles. Words like *focus* and *purpose* and *priorities* float through our conversations. Maybe it's age or perhaps it's the changing times, but we're more interested in harnessing energy to do a few things well, rather than accomplishing everything that somebody "out there" expects of us and rewarding ourselves with emotional breakdowns.

That's not easy for a goal-driven person like me. But as I focus deeper instead of wider and allow for who I am instead of who I think I should be, I'm happier and healthier. The number of my unfulfilled expectations and internal frustrations keeps diminishing. And it's rejuvenated my relationship with God because I'm learning to do what He asks of me and to set aside the rest.

Shakespeare wrote that "expectations often fail where there are many promises" (my translation).[2] Society promises us that we can do everything, without considering who God made each of us to be and what He's asked us to do. Society's promises fail. It's not physically possible for anyone to "have it all" and to succeed at everything.

On the other hand, the Bible says, "This is what the LORD your God wants you to do: Respect the LORD your God, and do what he has told you to do. Love him. Serve the LORD your God with your whole being, and obey the LORD's command" (Deuteronomy 10:12-13). God's promises never fail. He will fulfill His purpose for each of us (Psalm 138:8), if we're willing to seek and follow it.

When we set our goals to do what God wants us to do, we no longer need to be Superwoman. We can follow His blueprint for us, and with His plans, we can suceed.

PERSONAL CHECKPOINT

1. Could too many expectations be frustrating you and exhausting your effectiveness? Why, or why not?

2. Do any of your expectations originate from society's ideals? How do you feel about these expectations?

GOD'S VIEWPOINT

From the wise writer of Proverbs:

> *People may make plans in their minds,*
> *but only the LORD can make them come true.*
> *You may believe you are doing right,*
> *but the LORD will judge your reasons.*
> *Depend on the LORD in whatever you do,*
> *and your plans will succeed.*
> *The LORD makes everything go as he pleases.*
>
> *Love and truth bring forgiveness of sin.*
> *By respecting the LORD you will avoid evil.*
> *When people live so that they please the LORD,*
> *even their enemies will make peace with them.*
> *It is better to be poor and right*
> *than to be wealthy and dishonest.*

People may make plans in their minds,
  but the LORD decides what they will do.
The words of a king are like a message from God,
  so his decisions should be fair.

It is better to get wisdom than gold,
  and to choose understanding rather than silver!
Good people stay away from evil.
  By watching what they do, they protect their lives.
Pride will destroy a person;
  a proud attitude leads to ruin.
It is better to be humble and be with those who suffer
  than to share stolen property with the proud.
Whoever listens to what is taught will succeed,
  and whoever trusts the LORD will be happy.
                    —Proverbs 16:1-4, 6-10, 16-20

YOUR RESPONSE

1. How can you discover what God wants you to do and align yourself with these expectations?

2. Are you willing to let go of unfulfilled desires that may not be part of God's plan for you? Explain.

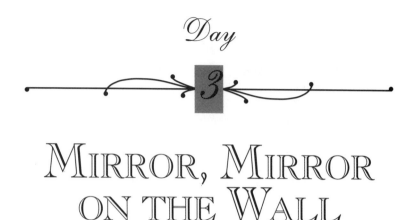

MIRROR, MIRROR ON THE WALL

*We can expect too much from the body
and not enough from the eternal spirit.*

*M*irror, mirror on the wall, who's got the fairest breasts of all?

For the past few years, this question has loomed large (pardon the pun) in the minds of American women. With the marketing and ban of silicone breast implants, what women carry upfront has obsessed the media, the medical community and, of course, women themselves.

In the least likely places, women are discussing mammary glands.

Recently, I delayed an all-day meeting that I was supposed to lead. So the group—all women from their late twenties to mid-forties—chatted while waiting for me.

Later I asked my assistant, "What did the women talk about while they waited?"

"Breasts."

"What?"

"You know . . . breasts," she answered again.

"Breasts?"

"Yeah. The size, the shape—that kind of stuff."

And these were committed Christian women.

*A*ctually, the current obsession with breasts isn't new. For centuries, women have scrutinized their chests for reassurance of their femininity. And more often than not, we've felt disappointed with what we see. Somehow, when it concerns our breasts, our perspective gets distorted. They're either too small, too big, too low, too uneven, or too something else.

Even my mother, who's consistently reluctant to talk about her body, once admitted, "When I was young, I always felt embarrassed about my breasts. They were too big." But looking at photos of Mom in her twenties, I see a body that women today spend millions of dollars to achieve: a voluptuous chest, thin arms, a tiny waist, slender legs. And I doubt that, strolling along a street with Mom, my dad felt any hint of humiliation.

And that brings up men. A good portion of our expectations about breasts pivots on *their* expectations about breasts. When Marie Antoinette traveled from Austria to meet her fiancé, the future Louis XVI of France, the elder king, Louis XV, sent a courtier to greet her party at the French border. The courtier then galloped his horse back to Louis XV to report on the bride.

The elder Louis immediately asked, "What do you think of her? Has she any bosom?" [3]

In the end, it's tragic how much emphasis we place on female body parts that God ordained for each woman. Just ask a woman with a mastectomy. She'd say any kind of breasts would be better than none at all.

*T*hat's the problem with too much expectation about body parts. We lose touch with the fact that, compared to many people, we're fortunate to have them, especially if they're in good working order.

Now don't take this wrong. Attention to health and fitness is good. Obsession with body shape is not good. It's anti-biblical. The psalmist praised God, saying, "You made me in an amazing and wonderful way. What you have done is wonderful" (Psalm 139:14). I'm sure God would appreciate our concentrating more on what's wonderful about His creation than on society's distorted standard for bodily perfection.

Even more, God wants us to nurture what's inside of us: the eternal spirit. No amount of leg lifts can compensate for a crabby and corrupt soul. And it's not our leotards that attract others to Christ or prepare a home for us in heaven.

PERSONAL CHECKPOINT

1. Are you disappointed with any part(s) of your body? If so, why?

2. On what do you base these bodily expectations?

GOD'S VIEWPOINT

A description of the body's nature and use:

We have this treasure from God, but we are like clay jars that hold the treasure. This shows that the great power is from God, not from us. We have troubles all around us, but we are not defeated. We do not know what to do, but we do not give up the hope of living.

Our physical body is becoming older and weaker, but our spirit inside us is made new every day. We have small troubles for a while now, but they are helping us gain an eternal glory that is much greater than the troubles. We set our eyes not on what we see, but on what we cannot see. What we see will last only a short time, but what we cannot see will last forever.

We know that our body—the tent we live in here on earth—will be destroyed. But when that happens, God will have a house for us. It will not be a house made by human hands; instead, it will be a home in heaven that will last forever. But now we groan in this tent. We want God to give us our heavenly home, because it will clothe us so we will not be naked. While we live in this body, we have burdens, and we groan. We do not want to be naked, but we want to be clothed with our heavenly home. Then this body that dies will be fully covered with life. This is what God made us for, and he has given us the Spirit to be a guarantee for this new life.

—2 Corinthians 4:7-8, 16b-18; 5:1-5

YOUR RESPONSE

1. How can you bring expectations about your body into God's perspective?

2. How can you begin to nurture your spirit more?

Day

4

NOBODY GOT THE PERFECT PRINCE

Men can't fill an internal gap that only God's Spirit can satisfy.

*A*t one time, the satirist Dorothy Parker worked alone in a small office in the Metropolitan Opera House in New York City. She got lonely and depressed because few people visited her there.

Then one day, a signwriter visited Dorothy to paint her name on the office's outside door. Thinking about her solitude, Dorothy convinced him otherwise. The signwriter painted the word, GENTLEMEN. [4]

I have friends who would have *loved* to hang out a sign titled "Gentlemen" and then watch men walk rather urgently toward them. I'm sure these women would have placed an event like that in the category of Dream Come True. However, most of us have grown to expect the men in our lives to arrive intermittently, with noticeable pauses and some coaxing in between.

Of course, that's only until Prince Charming appears, whom we marry and live with happily ever after. Right?

Well, sort of . . . and not always.

 $\mathcal{T}$ he same friends would say their men didn't turn out as princely as they'd hoped. More than once I've listened to a woman haltingly say, "You know, my husband (boyfriend) isn't who I thought he'd be." But unless he's abusive or entrenched in other harmful acts, that admission no longer alarms me. Discovering a man's fallibility sets the foundation for a real—and realistic—relationship. It seems that every couple needs an "awakening time" to plunge them into a more meaningful, life-lasting union.

Still, there's another statement I've heard more than once, and it's scary each time I hear it. It's when a woman says, "I lean on my husband (boyfriend) more than I depend on God." (Actually, she doesn't have to *say* this to decipher that she's *doing* it.) That's when she ignores her mandate to love God more than anyone else and to avoid idols (Deuteronomy 5: 9; 6:5).

Idols?

Well, yes. If idols are things that supersede God in our lives, then a lot of us trod shaky ground in regard to our men. But it's not just married women. We all know single women who would rather die than stay unmarried. Unfortunately, women who wave the A-Man-Or-I'll-Die banner are trying to plug an internal gap that only God's Spirit can fill.

When we place godlike expectations on men—when we want them to make up for what's missing inside of us—they can't help but disappoint us. God formed them from the earth's dust, and in the way of all idols, they will eventually crumble. With this in mind, we can place men where they rightfully belong: not above us, not below us, but alongside us as partners in living.

Ironically, when we give up our great expectations for and about men, everybody relaxes and our relationships with them improve. In a sense, we've let God be God and men be men—and we reap the benefit from both. That's not to say we condone childish or chauvinistic behavior from men; rather, we make room for their humanity. Because as far as I can tell, in marriage or in other relationships with males, nobody got the perfect prince.

 $\mathcal{I}$ t's fortunate, though, that men aren't perfect, because women aren't flawless, either. In male-female relationships, we need to forgive and forget a lot of personal junk from the opposite sex.

It's painful to relate to people who deny the pangs of humanity and, consequently, don't understand or allow for our imperfections. Women often complain about this in men. But when we heap unrealistic expectations for princeliness on males, aren't we doing the same to them?

Someday over lunch I'd love to hear one of us say, "You know, when I quit expecting him to make up for what's wrong with me, our relationship became more satisfying."

So far, I'm still waiting.

PERSONAL CHECKPOINT

1. What are your expectations for the men in your life?

2. Any chance you're expecting men to fill a gap that only God can satisfy?

GOD'S VIEWPOINT

Moses gave God's command to the Israelites:

You must not worship or serve any idol, because I, the LORD your God, am a jealous God.

These are the commands, rules, and laws that the LORD your God told me to teach you to obey in the land you are crossing the Jordan River to take. You, your children, and your grandchildren must respect the LORD your God as long as you live. Obey all his rules and commands I give you so that you will live a long time. Listen, Israel, and carefully obey these laws.

Listen, people of Israel! The LORD our God is the only LORD. Love the LORD your God with all your heart, all your soul, and all your strength. Always remember these commands I give you today. Teach them to your children, and talk about them when you sit at home and walk along the road, when you lie down and when you get up.

—*Deuteronomy 5:9; 6:1-3a, 4-7*

Paul warned the Colossians:

As you received Christ Jesus the Lord, so continue to live in him. Keep your roots deep in him and have your lives built on him. Be strong in the faith, just as you were taught, and always be thankful.

Be sure that no one leads you away with false and empty teaching that is only human, which comes from the ruling spirits of this world, and not from Christ. All of God lives in Christ fully (even when Christ was on earth), and you have a full and true life in Christ, who is ruler over all rulers and powers.

So do not let anyone make rules for you about eating and drinking or about a religious feast, a New Moon Festival, or a Sabbath day.

They do not hold tightly to Christ, the head. It is from him that all the parts of the body are cared for and held together. So it grows in the way God wants it to grow.

—Colossians 2:6-10, 16, 19

YOUR RESPONSE

1. How can you determine if you love God as He asked us to love Him?

2. How could loving God above everyone else affect your expectations about men?

Day

5

HI HO, IT'S OFF TO WORK WE GO

When we expect work to substitute for character, we wind up feeling empty.

Clare Boothe Luce grabbed for everything she could squeeze out of life and accomplishments. Born in the tenements, at an early age Clare vowed to abandon obscurity and become memorable through her work and associations.

That she did. In the 1930s, she rose to managing editor of *Vanity Fair.* Through her later marriage to Henry Luce, she influenced the man who created the TIME, INC., publishing empire. Together, they grew powerfully rich.

But for Clare, that wasn't enough. After stints in magazine publishing, she also wrote much-acclaimed plays, served two terms in Congress, and became the United States ambassador to Italy. Clare's work accomplishments labeled her "a woman ahead of her time." And to top it off, she fashionably displayed her beautiful face and figure.

To the public, there wasn't anything Clare couldn't do, nothing she didn't own. In private, her friends and family observed that she relentlessly pursued what she never achieved: inner peace.

Clare competed against Henry for fame and resented his control over the business. She ignored her daughter and collected enemies almost as fast as she engaged in love affairs with intriguing men. She suffered paranoid depressions and thwarted Henry's attempts at divorce when their marriage shriveled because of her selfishness.

For Clare, possessing more than anyone else was never enough.

"One achieves so much less than one's expectations," she said toward the end of her life. "I was thinking at one time of writing my memoirs and calling it, 'Confessions of an Unsuccessful Woman.' I've done too many things and it doesn't stack up." [5]

*H*ow can a woman achieve so much and still feel unsuccessful? It's not because she shouldn't be working. Just as He did with Adam and Eve in the Garden, God gives us jobs to complete. Innately, we feel a person should work at something. Even if we don't like the kind of work she chooses or how she accomplishes it or the fact that she doesn't get paid for it. We want to know, "What, exactly, does that woman *do?*"

But where a woman works isn't the real crippler, either. Whether she works in the home, in the marketplace, or in both isn't what undergirds or undermines her satisfaction. Nor is it the number of accomplishments and kudos she acquires. It's who that woman is *being* while she works.

Is she the kind of person God asks her to be? This is the most important question—and it's much more difficult to answer. This question addresses her character.

I used to hate the word *being*. I couldn't codify it, wrap my arms around it, or admire it framed and hanging on a wall. And if I couldn't show it off in a tangible way, I wasn't much interested in it. However, that changed when I reached the law of diminishing returns with my work. I collected more and more accomplishments and felt less and less satisfied with them. It was as if I'd dropped them into a bottomless hole inside of me, only to feel endlessly empty.

That's when a friend timidly ventured, "Judy, who are you *being?* Maybe you need to work on who you are more than what you do."

I took that comment as an insult, but eventually took it to heart. (Sometimes we need a jolt to change direction and save the soul.) I believed wholeheartedly that I was following God's purpose for my life—that I was doing the work He created me to do. But I'd omitted the other half of the spiritual equation. Through my work, God wanted me to express His character: to be who He wanted me to be.

I wish I could say that now I'm transformed and always feel more concerned about building my character than my résumé. That fact is, *being* starts a lifelong process of learning the hard way. The most difficult decisions of our careers emerge when we begin valuing character more than conquests in the workplace.

The marketplace expects us to prove our worth by our work. God wants us to be worthy women of character. At the end of our lives, the difference between these two will determine how things stack up for us.

Personal Checkpoint

1. What are your expectations for work at home or in the marketplace?

2. At work, how does your *being* compare to your *doing*?

God's Viewpoint

About the working woman in Proverbs:

> She looks for wool and flax
> and likes to work with her hands.
> She is like a trader's ship,
> bringing food from far away.
> She gets up while it is still dark
> and prepares food for her family
> and feeds her servant girls.
> She inspects a field and buys it.
> With money she earned, she plants a vineyard.

She does her work with energy,
and her arms are strong.
She knows that what she makes is good.
Her lamp burns late into the night.
She makes thread with her hands
and weaves her own cloth.
She welcomes the poor
and helps the needy.
She does not worry about her family when it snows,
because they all have fine clothes to keep them warm.
She makes coverings for herself;
her clothes are made of linen and other expensive
material.
She makes linen clothes and sells them
and provides belts to the merchants.
She is strong and is respected by the people.
She looks forward to the future with joy.
She speaks wise words
and teaches others to be kind.
She watches over her family
and never wastes her time.
Her children speak well of her.
Her husband also praises her,
saying, "There are many fine women,
but you are better than all of them."
Charm can fool you, and beauty can trick you,
but a woman who respects the LORD should be
praised.
Give her the reward she has earned;
she should be praised in public for what she has
done.

—Proverbs 31:13-22, 24-31

YOUR RESPONSE

1. How does this ideal working woman balance *doing* with *being*?

2. What helpful insights could this woman bring to your less-than-ideal workplace?

WHERE ARE THE EMPEROR'S CLOTHES?

***If we expect leaders to be flawless,
they'll disappoint us.***

But the emperor is naked," the little boy whispered to his father.

Startled, the father looked at his son, then at the emperor parading by his subjects. Perhaps the boy was right.

The father had heard stories about their leader's ridiculous obsession with clothes. How the emperor would rather spend time admiring his clothes closet than inspecting the soldiers, attending the theater, or any other of his duties. And how, lately, two weavers had captured the emperor's undivided attention and deep financial pockets with their promise of sewing him splendid garments, unlike any in the world.

According to the weavers, the cloth they created for the emperor looked extraordinarily beautiful, but it also held strange powers. It was invisible to anyone unfit for office or unforgivably stupid.

If I owned that cloth, then I'd know which of my councilors were unfit for their jobs—and I could pick out the clever ones for myself, the emperor thought. Then he gave the weavers money, fine silk, and gold thread so they could begin creating their masterpiece.

After a while, the emperor felt curious about the weavers' progress, but he felt reluctant to visit their shop for fear he'd see nothing on the looms and prove his own stupidity. Instead, he commissioned his faithful prime minister to inspect the work and to report on its appearance.

By then, the townspeople had heard of the cloth's magical powers and eagerly awaited finding out, as they suspected, that their neighbors were unfit or unintelligent. The prime minister felt the pressure as he hurried to the shop. If so many people believed, then he'd believe, too.

Upon arrival, the old prime minister witnessed the weavers furiously at work, but he saw nothing on the looms. Afraid of losing his job, he adjusted his glasses and exclaimed, "What a beautiful cloth! What patterns and colors!" He reported the same to the emperor.

*A*t this point, the emperor felt he possessed a new way to test his staff's competency. He sent another trusted councilor to the shop, and fearing stupidity, the man also described a magnificent piece of cloth to his excellency. The weavers increased their amount of time at the looms—and the number of coins and supplies they needed to accomplish the task.

Finally, the emperor visited the shop himself.

Oh, no, it's just as I feared, he thought while scrutinizing the loom again and again. *I'm unfit to be the ruler of this kingdom. But I don't need to let anyone know.* The emperor asked the weavers to cut the imaginary cloth into trousers, a royal robe and a train—and agreed to wear them at a grand procession through town.

"This material is so light, it feels like a spider's web," said the swindling weavers as the emperor pretended to put on his new outfit. Those around him agreed, and commented on its great beauty. By now, the emperor felt so much pressure not to disappoint his subjects he swallowed his dismay and continued the charade.

Two gentlemen of the imperial bedchamber fumbled to pick up the imaginary train as the emperor exited the palace to the cheers of an adoring crowd. . . . [6]

*S*ometimes, our expectations for leaders are so unrealistic they can't help but disappoint us. Sometimes, those expectations disguise a fear of ourselves. And sometimes, we shouldn't follow leaders because they do stupid things.

It's our responsibility to discern—and realistically respond to—the options.

✿

PERSONAL CHECKPOINT

1. What expectations do you have for spiritual leaders? Are these expectations realistic?

2. How do you feel about following a flawed spiritual leader?

GOD'S VIEWPOINT

Realistic instructions for God's people:

God chose you to be his people, so I urge you now to live the life to which God called you. Always be humble, gentle, and patient, accepting each other in love. You are joined together with peace through the Spirit, so make every effort to continue together in this way. There is one body and one Spirit, and God called you to have one hope. There is one Lord, one faith, and one baptism. There is one God and Father of everything. He rules everything and is everywhere and is in everything.

Christ gave each one of us the special gift of grace, showing how generous he is. That is why it says in the Scriptures,

"When he went up to the heights,
he led a parade of captives,
and he gave gifts to people."

And Christ gave gifts to people—he made some to be apostles, some to be prophets, some to go and tell the Good News, and some to have the work of caring for and teaching God's people. Christ gave those gifts to prepare God's holy people for the work of serving, to make the body of Christ stronger. This work must continue until we are all joined together in the same faith and in the same knowledge of the Son of God. We must become like a mature person, growing until we become like Christ and have his perfection.

Then we will no longer be babies. We will not be tossed about like a ship that the waves carry one way and then another. We will not be influenced by every new teaching we hear from people who are trying to fool us. They make plans and try any kind of trick to fool people into following the wrong path. No! Speaking the truth with love, we will grow up in every way into Christ, who is the head. The whole body depends on Christ, and all the parts of the body are joined and held together. Each part does its own work to make the whole body grow and be strong with love.

In the Lord's name, I tell you this. Do not continue living like those who do not believe. Their thoughts are worth nothing. They do not understand, and they know nothing, because they refuse to listen. So they cannot have the life that God gives.

—Ephesians 4:1b-8, 11-18

YOUR RESPONSE

1. How can you discern whom to choose as your spiritual leader?

2. When allowing for a leader's humanity, how far is too far?

Part Two

CAUGHT IN THE REALITY GAP

When your life and expectations don't meet

*A*s long as we writers (and speakers) tout our successes and gloss over our failures, we perpetuate the myth that if one is committed in faith, vigilant in relationships, organized in habits, positive in outlook . . . the good life is well nigh inevitable. The real woman who is living in the trenches begins to think that others succeed where she alone fails. She looks at the bookshelves and imagines a composite woman who can do it all, while she can do hardly anything.

She may come to believe she is unique in her disappointments and failures. A suspicion of inadequacy creeps into her life, and with it comes isolation. Unable to articulate her frustrations, she becomes vaguely disconcerted and increasingly alone with her problems.[7]

Alice Slaikeu Lawhead,
The Lie of the Good Life

I picked up the glass on my office desk and hurled it at the wall. As shattered bits spread across the carpet, I choked, "This is insanity! Is this what I get for following You, God?"

I slumped to the floor and sobbed. My dreams were smoldering, and I wanted to join the ashes. Just a few nights before I'd driven to the ocean with thoughts of wading in permanently. But imagining a grief-stricken family and greeting my own cowardice stopped me. So there I sat, in a dim office late at night, angry and afraid.

After a while, the tears dried and my sobs dwindled to a silent moan. I pulled myself upright, and in my exhausted, mixed-up thinking, I felt more alarmed by a fresh dent in the wall than my death wish. Dropping to the floor again, I shakily picked up bits of glass, hoping to remove any evidence so colleagues wouldn't ask questions the next morning.

I had started with good intentions. Several years before, I'd resigned a secular job and, convinced of the Lord's leading, left family and friends to enter Christian work two states away. Friends felt unanimous: the move wonderfully combined my talents, training, and desire to serve God. I left for the new job excited and purposeful.

Soon after, life crumbled. I hated my job and apartment. It was tough finding friends outside of work. I'd taken a salary cut and my money dwindled. My car disintegrated at the rate of a few hundred dollars each month. A potential romance fizzled. I developed health problems. I felt lonely.

After a few years, though, circumstances improved and I began to ask God for my dream job. The hope of that ultimate goal had helped me to persevere, and now that I'd "paid my dues," I felt certain God would answer my request and bless me. So months later, it delighted me to finally sense God's go-ahead on a position with another company.

Unfortunately, this new job dropped me to my knees, scuttling for broken bits of glass, searching for fragments of myself. After eight months of employment, the company terminated my job. I felt stranded: no job in sight, no money or family to fall back on, no emotional reserve to cope, no trust that God would rescue me. Caught in the gap between my dreams and reality, I thought the Lord had abandoned me.

With hindsight, I know that God didn't forsake me. In fact, I can trace how He worked behind the scenes for my eventual good. But that night, nobody could have convinced me of His care or presence.

*W*hen we discover that life and our expectations don't meet, it's difficult to look past the pain toward anything better. And for a while, we need permission to feel the emotions of the reality gap. The reality gap is that unwanted space between what we want life to be and what it has actually become.

Landing in this gap can feel devastating, but it doesn't have to destroy us. Rather, we can use the disappointment to evaluate, re-direct, and motivate us toward better living, even the fulfillment of our dreams. But first we need emergency aid and reassurance after the crash landing. And that begins by leaning into God's welcoming arms.

❦

PERSONAL CHECKPOINT

Part Two can help you seek God's help as you reckon with the reality gap.

1. What is the nature of your reality gap?

2. How does it feel to land in this gap?

3. How do you feel toward God?

You Can Trust Your Feelings

***Emotions can reveal our soul's condition
while we're waiting for God's answers.***

slumped back in the church pew as the youth group
leader scrawled and squeaked a diagram on the chalk-
board. *If I've seen that diagram once, I've seen it a thousand times,* I
thought, borrowing and editing my mother's favorite retort when
she was disgusted with daughters who didn't listen.

The phrase fit the moment because I felt annoyed, too. No,
maybe I felt more dismayed. Or apathetic. Yes, apathetic
described me nicely. Some time ago, I'd passed frustration and
anguish. For the sake of my teenaged life, I couldn't align with
this drawing that, once again, emerged at a Bible-study lesson.
And I felt tired of trying.

So I reluctantly eyed each of the three "cars" that formed a
yellow, chalky "train" on the board in front of me. He'd boldly
titled the train's engine with the word FACT. This was the most
important train car because it provided the power to pull the others. Spiritually speaking, this meant we needed to center our lives
firmly on biblical facts.

This was fine by me. In my first decade, I'd garnered several
perfect-attendance pins and out-quoted every kid at Sunday

school, three years in a row, to win the Scripture memory contest. I knew plenty of facts—and I believed them.

The second train car just sat there, holding two other cars together. However, for spiritual application, our leader marked it FAITH. He said this car held deep meaning for our small band of half-listening learners. He told us that, after basing our spiritual walk on the facts, we needed to exercise faith.

Faith sounded okay by me, too. Yet it somehow always eluded me. In the last year, I'd believed myself peppy enough to join the drill team, but this honor had embraced other young women. Still, I had faith in the faith car. I knew faith ushered me into God's Kingdom, and it seemed I'd always believed that. It was the day-to-day stuff that needed working out.

It was the inevitable third car—the caboose—that continually baffled me. Once again, I faced its title: FEELING. Our youth group leader, who often expressed volatile feelings, said, "To be a growing Christian, we must put away our feelings and depend on facts and faith." The implication: Don't trust feelings, especially if they affect your relationship with God. They're unreliable and bad. We're carnal to give in to them.

The man might as well have told me to stop breathing. Descended from generations of creative people on my maternal family tree, I'd inherited the passionate, sensitive nature of artistic relatives who'd felt their way through life before me.

Years later, a friend lovingly told me, "Judy, your antenna is always out, sensing and feeling your way through everything." My friend considered this a powerful attribute for an author. But sitting on a hard pew that Sunday night, I hadn't lived long enough to confirm her wisdom.

What could I do? No matter how much I struggled against them, I couldn't obliterate my feelings, so I called myself a bad Christian.

More than two decades later, the fear of feelings still haunts believers. We admire those who keep emotions in check to rationally face doubts and difficulties; we describe them as godly and courageous. On the other hand, we attribute feelings to undisciplined men, weak-willed women, and people from other denominations. We long to stand strong and unflinching in our faith; we fear that feelings might point to our weaknesses.

When we approach Christianity this way, we tilt God's upside-down kingdom back to a position that's more secular than saintly. Certainly, facts and faith play a fundamental role in our spiritual journey. But feelings merit a place, too. God created us with the capacity to feel joy, pain, anger, pleasure, and other emotions. He created us in His image; He gets emotional, too. He feels joy over worship, pain for sin, anger toward waywardness, and pleasure from creation. He remains an example of purely motivated and honestly expressed feelings.

Unfortunately, the fall of humanity ushered in sin-based emotions that don't resemble God's feelings: shame, fear, guilt, bitterness, and others. Some say these emotions should take no part in a Christian's daily walk. But only a glance around tells us differently.

Even though Christ's blood rendered us perfect in God's eyes, we still live in decaying bodies in a sinful world. And whether or not we admit it, we bring muddled minds, wounded spirits, and withered souls to the Cross. Through sanctification, Christ renews and reshapes us into His likeness, but it's a lifelong, up-and-down process. To believe otherwise forces us into denial.

So when unmet expectations erupt in raging feelings, we can dump our doubts and dysfunctions, weaknesses and humiliations, at Christ's feet. We can admit our sin-based problems, which often reveal themselves through erupting emotions. We can trust our feelings to measure the condition of our souls. And instead of denying our feelings to appear spiritual, we can confront them to find healing.

PERSONAL CHECKPOINT

1. In relationship to your unmet expectations, what feelings do you struggle against?

2. Do these feelings indicate anything about your soul's condition?

GOD'S VIEWPOINT

What Jesus taught about feelings:

> *Those people who know they have great spiritual needs are happy,*
> *because the kingdom of heaven belongs to them.*
> *Those who are sad now are happy,*
> *because God will comfort them.*
> *Those who are humble are happy,*
> *because the earth will belong to them.*
> *Those who want to do right more than anything else are happy,*
> *because God will fully satisfy them.*
> *Those who show mercy to others are happy,*
> *because God will show mercy to them.*
> *Those who are pure in their thinking are happy,*
> *because they will be with God.*
> *Those who work to bring peace are happy,*
> *because God will call them his children.*
> *Those who are treated badly for doing good are happy,*
> *because the kingdom of heaven belongs to them.*
> *—Matthew 5:3-10*

YOUR RESPONSE

1. In the above passage, other translations of the Bible use the word *blessed* instead of *happy*. What do these two words reveal about Christ's response when we feel the emotions of life's disappointments?

2. How can you be assured of God's blessing when the emotions of unmet desires overwhelm you?

WHERE DID GOD GO?

*He encompasses us in every moment
and situation, even when life hurts.*

During World War II, the Nazis arrested two men and threw them into a room with a boy. All three males were Jewish, and wondered about their destiny.

They didn't have to worry for long. Soon German soldiers entered the room and hung the boy in front of the others. Tragically, the boy didn't weigh enough to die quickly. It took thirty minutes for life to choke out of him.

As the older men watched the boy's agonizing death, one of them asked the other, "Where is God now?"

"Right here. With us," answered his companion. [8]

Where is God when it hurts? When senseless events turn life upside down and evil wins? When we beg and plead, and God still keeps us waiting for a miracle? According to the Bible, God is "all around" us, in front and behind us (Psalm 139:5).

When I first heard about the young boy hanging in front of his elders, I found that concept hard to believe. If God accompanied these men, why didn't He do something? After all, He's the

God of miracles. He could have obliterated the Nazis. He could have rescued the men.

Why does He allow such evil?

I don't know the answer. It's a question that's puzzled theologians for centuries. They've talked about humanity's free will, too little faith, too much sin, and Satan's roam of the earth. Still, I wonder why the All-Powerful delays His answers to people's prayers and leaves them defenseless.

I believe the ultimate answer will stay hidden among the mysteries of faith until, someday in eternity, God reveals His reasons. But even with this explanation, I'm assuming that the God of the Universe—the One who hangs the stars on nothing—must account to me, the one who can't hang clothes straight in a closet. When really, God will unfold what He chooses to reveal at His appointed time. And because He wants to—not because I shake my finger at Him with disgust.

When I remember my place in the world compared to God's sovereignty over it, I lower my hand. My finite mind cannot grasp the infinite plans of the Alpha and Omega, the beginning and the end. But my heart can soak in His love and compassion. And here's where I uncover comfort in this tragic war story.

God did not abandon those suffering men. He hovered all around them, comforting, strengthening, even grieving with them. And one of them chose to believe in His presence, despite the circumstances. Instead of shaking his fist with bitterness, he opened his arms to love.

Not an easy choice. Yet it's a decision we can make when life hurts and it feels like God has forgotten us. Instead of always asking *Why?* we can ask *Where?* and discover God all around us, longing to comfort and console us.

Even in darkness, He is there, waiting for us to reach out.

Personal Checkpoint

1. What causes you to ask, "Where is God?"

2. How do you feel when God seems to abandon you?

GOD'S VIEWPOINT

A prayer recognizing God's presence:

> LORD, *you have examined me*
> *and know all about me.*
> *You know when I sit down and when I get up.*
> *You know my thoughts before I think them.*
> *You know where I go and where I lie down.*
> *You know thoroughly everything I do.*
> LORD, *even before I say a word,*
> *you already know it.*
> *You are all around me—in front and in back—*
> *and have put your hand on me.*
> *Your knowledge is amazing to me;*
> *it is more than I can understand.*
>
> *Where can I go to get away from your Spirit?*
> *Where can I run from you?*
> *If I go up to the heavens, you are there.*
> *If I lie down in the grave, you are there.*
> *If I rise with the sun in the east*
> *and settle in the west beyond the sea,*
> *even there you would guide me.*
> *With your right hand you would hold me.*
>
> *I could say, "The darkness will hide me.*
> *Let the light around me turn into night."*
> *But even the darkness is not dark to you.*
> *The night is as light as the day;*
> *darkness and light are the same to you.*
>
> *You made my whole being;*
> *you formed me in my mother's body.*
> *I praise you because you made me in an amazing*
> *and wonderful way.*
> *What you have done is wonderful.*
> *I know this very well.*
> *You saw my bones being formed*
> *as I took shape in my mother's body.*

When I was put together there,
*   you saw my body as it was formed.*
All the days planned for me
*   were written in your book*
*   before I was one day old.*

God, your thoughts are precious to me.
*   They are so many!*
If I could count them,
*   they would be more than all the grains of sand.*
When I wake up,
*   I am still with you.*

God, I wish you would kill the wicked!
*   Get away from me, you murderers!*
They say evil things about you.
*   Your enemies use your name thoughtlessly.*
LORD, I hate those who hate you;
*   I hate those who rise up against you.*
I feel only hate for them;
*   they are my enemies.*

God, examine me and know my heart;
*   test me and know my nervous thoughts.*
See if there is any bad thing in me.
*   Lead me on the road to everlasting life.*
*   —Psalm 139*

YOUR RESPONSE

1. How can God be "all around" us?

2. How can you become aware of His constant presence?

THE BAD, THE WORSE, THE UGLY

God can deliver us from the sin that thwarts our dreams.

ou're so selfish! You never listen to what I say! I've done all of this work for you, and you don't even care!"

"Oh, yeah? Well, you're just too demanding! Everybody says you're awfully hard to work for!"

"Don't throw that 'everybody' stuff at me! I dare you to name names . . ."

Two angry, accusatory voices ricocheted down the office halls. And one of them was mine.

I'd known this committee meeting might be difficult, but I hadn't expected the surprising turn it took, leaving me dismayed and defenseless. For the last hour of the agenda, I'd felt my anger building toward the chairperson, but managed to stave it off. Now, with everybody gone but us, we verbally ripped into each other like blood-hungry wildcats.

So much for my professionalism. It was the worst fight of my life: a yelling, fist-pounding confrontation. And I was too tired, too overworked, to care about how this battle would damage me, my co-worker, and our relationship.

That is, until I tossed in bed that night, tearfully blinking at the darkness. Then I accused myself: *Why in the world did I behave that way? I must be a horrible person to yell like that. Why can't I act the way I want to?*

I'd really wanted to serve on this committee: I'd hoped it would advance me professionally. But agonizing alone in the dark, I realized that my sinful demands for control were torching that goal.

*I*t's been said that "adversities do not make the person either weak or strong, but they reveal what he is."[9] That's not a comforting thought when inward pressures turn into less-than-admirable actions. It's painful to lose control and not act the way we really want to. Especially when these actions keep us from fulfilling our dreams.

During those times, we'd rather do most anything than peer inside and greet the bad, the worse, and the ugly about ourselves.

Interestingly enough, it's not just the knockout fights, the damaging faux pas, that can shame us. From bingeing on food to hurting our children, we're frustrated when we fail to do the "right" thing, when no matter how hard we try, our actions don't reflect our good intentions.

Unfortunately, age and maturity don't always close the gap between who we are and who we'd like to be.

"You know, I've read that *who you really are* gets intensified as you grow older," a thirtysomething friend worried aloud to me. "That means the sweet people will get sweeter. But I'm afraid I'm going to be an unbearable old lady, because I can be so awful now!"

Of course, my friend can work on her actions. But she's hit on something that we all know: a polished exterior only camouflages an interior self that can be tricky to control. And it's the interior self that blocks us from our heart's desires.

*W*e may determine to change through self-discipline or with the help of counselors, but these efforts remain limited without looking at our spiritual selves and the sin that resides within us. When we unearth the causes for our problems, we find sin tangled in the roots.

LORD, HAVE YOU FORGOTTEN ME?

The good news is that God wants to rescue us from sin—and from the inability to trust ourselves and our actions. He can infuse us with His power so we can change and live fully. But first, we must admit and repent of the sin that binds us. We can depend on the promise that, if we confess our sin, God will hear and forgive us—and heal the shame that haunts us (1 John 1:9).

Without God's power to change me, I'd never have found forgiveness with the people I offended. With the ancient psalm writer I agree: "I would have despaired unless I had believed that I would see the goodness of the Lord" (Psalm 27:13; NASV).

And with that focus, we can begin changing our disappointing actions and moving toward our dreams. [10]

Personal Checkpoint

1. Could sin be hindering the fulfillment of your desires?

2. After confessing sin, could you also need healing from the hurt and shame it has caused?

God's Viewpoint

A prayer for confessing sin:

> God, be merciful to me
>   because you are loving.
> Because you are always ready to be merciful,
>   wipe out all my wrongs.
> Wash away all my guilt
>   and make me clean again.
>
> I know about my wrongs,
>   and I can't forget my sin.
> You are the only one I have sinned against;
>   I have done what you say is wrong.
> You are right when you speak
>   and fair when you judge.

I was brought into this world in sin.
  In sin my mother gave birth to me.

You want me to be completely truthful,
  so teach me wisdom.
Take away my sin, and I will be clean.
  Wash me, and I will be whiter than snow.
Make me hear sounds of joy and gladness;
  let the bones you crushed be happy again.
Turn your face from my sins
  and wipe out all my guilt.

Create in me a pure heart, God,
  and make my spirit right again.
Do not send me away from you
  or take your Holy Spirit from me.
Give me back the joy of your salvation.
  Keep me strong by giving me a willing spirit.
Then I will teach your ways to those who do wrong,
  and sinners will turn back to you.

The sacrifice God wants is a broken spirit.
  God, you will not reject a heart that is broken and
    sorry for sin.
                                        —Psalm 51:1-13, 17

YOUR RESPONSE

1. After asking for God's forgiveness, what changes may you need to make to turn away from sin?

2. For you, is turning away from sin a one-time act or an ongoing process?

THE MYSTERY OF PAIN

**The pain from unfulfilled desires
can strengthen our wavering spirits.**

*I*n the story *The Jewel in the Crown,* blind Sister Ludmilla described a conversation she once had with God. They talked about the old woman's disabilities.

> "I'm sorry about your eyes," He said, "but there's nothing I can do unless you want a miracle."
>
> "No," [she] said, "no miracle, thank You. I shall get used to it and I expect you will help me.
>
> "Anyway, when you've lived a long time and can hardly hobble about on sticks and spend most of the day in bed, your eyes aren't much use. I would need three miracles, one for the eyes, one for the legs, and one to take twenty years off my age!
>
> "Three miracles for one old woman! What a waste! Besides . . . miracles are to convince the unconvinced. What do you take me for? An unbeliever?" [11]

Earlier in her life, Sister Ludmilla had directed and funded a hostel for the poor. She'd nursed the sick, the dying, the hungry.

And it never occurred to her that because she followed the Master she'd be shielded from affliction. She simply kept believing and serving.

However we feel about Sister Ludmilla's theology concerning miracles, there's a lesson in her attitude about pain. She accepted the mysterious fact that God doesn't exempt His children from suffering.

We're not living in the environment that our Creator intended for us. Earthquakes, war, death, and other tragedies weren't included in His original, perfect plan. Neither were sickness, broken relationships, or the disappointments of unfulfilled desires. Heralds from a ravaged world, they remind us that, long ago, humans turned to their own way.

This doesn't mean God won't intervene and redeem painful situations. But neither will He completely exempt us from them. When we were "bought by God for a price" (1 Corinthians 6:20), the purchase came with no warranty against pain, no guarantee that following His will would produce a specified number of miracles. In fact, Christ promised us tribulation (John 16:33).

*F*or about a decade, I lived with unfulfilled desires that regularly dumped me into a slough of depression. During one bout of despair, I complained to a friend, "My life is so painful, what can I say to my non-Christian friends? Asking them to follow God feels like inviting them to suffer!"

While this friend sat quietly, the poignancy of my words sank in. According to the apostle Peter, *suffering is precisely what Christians are called to do.* In 1 Peter 2:19-21, he wrote to persecuted Christians: "A person might have to suffer even when it's unfair, but if he thinks of God and stands the pain, God is pleased. If you are beaten for doing wrong, there is no reason to praise you for being patient in your punishment. But if you suffer for doing good, and you are patient, then God is pleased. This is what you were called to do, because Christ suffered for you and gave you an example to follow. So you should do as he did."

Peter's readers suffered as believers living in a pagan culture. People like me suffer because we're Christians too often living like pagans. We're in pain from the sins of our parents, the sins of our community, the sins of ourselves. And Christ, longing to create His likeness in us, allows the suffering. He knows if we bow to its swordlike presence, we become more useful in His service.

Like no other aspect of life, pain teaches us a crash course in spiritual growth. Depending on our circumstances, God may allow the pain of unfulfilled desires for a number of reasons. For example, pain purges sin. It exposes our wounds so they can be healed. It refines our faith. It helps us to change for the better. It develops heartfelt compassion. It draws us closer to God. But despite our quest for answers, our orderly lists of reasons, the psalmist probably modeled the wisest approach to the problem of pain.

"Why am I so sad?" he asked. Then skipping the answer, he admonished himself: "I should put my hope in God and keep praising him, my savior and my God" (Psalm 42:5). He realized that *apparent* reasons for our pain often don't exist. Even if we're in God's will or spiritually mature or obedient in everything.

Ultimately, we're forced to skip the answers, to trust in God. For He—not a list of explanations—is our only hope. And we keep praising Him because the God of our difficulties is also the God of our deliverance.

It is, indeed, a mystery.

❧

Personal Checkpoint

1. What pain do you endure today?

2. How is pain connected to your unfulfilled desires?

God's Viewpoint

The psalmist searches for God:

> *As a deer thirsts for streams of water,*
> *so I thirst for you, God.*
> *I thirst for the living God.*
> *When can I go to meet with him?*
> *Day and night, my tears have been my food.*
> *People are always saying,*
> *"Where is your God?"*

When I remember these things,
 I speak with a broken heart.
I used to walk with the crowd
  and lead them to God's Temple
  with songs of praise.

Why am I so sad?
 Why am I so upset?
I should put my hope in God
  and keep praising him,
  my Savior and my God.

I am very sad.
 So I remember you where the Jordan River begins,
near the peaks of Hermon and Mount Mizar.
Troubles have come again and again, sounding like waterfalls.
 Your waves are crashing all around me.
The LORD shows his true love every day.
  At night I have a song,
  and I pray to my living God.
I say to God, my Rock,
  "Why have you forgotten me?
Why am I sad
  and troubled by my enemies?"
My enemies' insults make me feel
  as if my bones were broken.
They are always saying,
  "Where is your God?"

Why am I so sad?
 Why am I so upset?
I should put my hope in God
  and keep praising him,
  my Savior and my God.
                              —Psalm 42

YOUR RESPONSE

1. What good could result from your pain?

2. How can you keep trusting in God?

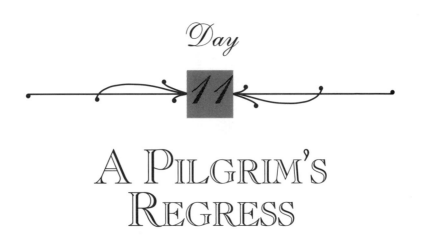
A PILGRIM'S REGRESS

*Unmet expectations can tempt us to backslide
and roadblock the fulfillment of our desires.*

ometimes, it's the old stories that most poignantly teach us about everyday survival. Especially when those stories address matters of the heart.

Take, for example, *The Pilgrim's Progress* by John Bunyan. In this classic allegory, Christian embarked on a treacherous journey toward the Celestial City. Just before entering the land of Beulah, Christian and his companion, Hopeful, discussed how some men backslide from walking in the [Holy] Spirit.

From *Pilgrim's Progress:*

Hopeful: Now I have showed you the reasons for their going back. Do you show me the manner thereof.
Christian: So I will willingly.

1. They draw off their thoughts, all that they may, from the remembrance of God, death, and judgment to come.

2. Then they cast off by degrees private duties, as closet prayer, curbing their lusts, watching, sorrow for sin, and the like.

3. Then they shun the company of lively and warm Christians.

4. After that they grow cold to public duty, as hearing, reading, godly conference, and the like.

5. Then they begin to pick holes, as we say, in the coats of some of the godly; and that devilishly, that they may have seeming colour to throw religion (for the sake of some infirmity they have spied in them) behind their backs.

6. They begin to adhere to and associate themselves with carnal, loose, and wanton men.

7. Then they give way to carnal and wanton discourses in secret; and glad are they if they can see such things in any that are counted honest that they may the more boldly do it through their example.

8. After this they begin to play with little sins openly.

9. And then, being hardened, they show themselves as they are. Thus, being launched again into the gulf of misery, unless a miracle of grace prevent it, they everlastingly perish on their own deceivings. [12]

Once we break past the seventeenth-century language, there's a warning in this passage for those of us who live with unfulfilled expectations. We can feel disappointed with God and gradually forsake Him.

A contemporary version of Christian's backsliding steps looks like this:

A thirty-eight-year-old woman feels bereft because God hasn't given her a husband.

1. She begins to think less about obeying God and more about satisfying her needs.

2. She stops praying and starts reading the steamy novels she loved before following Christ.

3. She stops socializing with women who have happy marriages.

4. She stops attending her small-group Bible study so she won't encounter married couples.

5. She begins mocking people who believe in family values and points out their weaknesses.

6. She starts running with her old, wild crowd of friends and flirting with the men.

7. She privately decides that, if God won't answer her prayers for a man, she'll at least start having an affair so she doesn't miss out on sex, too.

8. Later, she doesn't care who knows about her decision.

9. She begins an affair with a married man, figuring this is the best she'll ever get in life. The relationship is shaky and she's unhappy, but she won't admit it. She blames God for everything.

*W*hatever the circumstances, it's easy to embark on the road to spiritual defection when we feel disappointed with God. I've traveled that road myself and, after several years, I've learned that abandoning God doesn't solve anything. Ironically, it blocks Him from fulfilling our desires. And if we try to fulfill those desires on our own, the acquisition turns meaningless.

It's far better to feel "stuck" waiting on God than to plunge ahead into Satan's gulf of misery. (Besides, who knows? Maybe God's answer is only days away.) But if we've already begun the defector's journey, it's never too late to grab grace and turn back.

PERSONAL CHECKPOINT

1. What attitudes could begin a defection from God?

2. Do you feel tempted to fulfill your desires without God's help?

GOD'S VIEWPOINT

Praise from a person who kept waiting on God:

Come and see what God has done,
the amazing things he has done for people.

He turned the sea into dry land.
*   The people crossed the river on foot.*
*   So let us rejoice because of what he did.*
He rules forever with his power.
*   He keeps his eye on the nations,*
*   so people should not turn against him.*

You people, praise our God;
*   loudly sing his praise.*
He protects our lives
*   and does not let us be defeated.*
God you have tested us;
*   you have purified us like silver.*
You let us be trapped
*   and put a heavy load on us.*
You let our enemies walk on our heads.
*   We went through fire and flood,*
*   but you brought us to a place with good things.*

All of you who fear God, come and listen,
*   and I will tell you what he has done for me.*
I cried out to him with my mouth
*   and praised him with my tongue.*
If I had known of any sin in my heart,
*   the Lord would not have listened to me.*
But God has listened;
*   he has heard my prayer.*
Praise God,
*   who did not ignore my prayer*
*   or hold back his love from me.*
*   —Psalm 66: 5-12, 16-20*

YOUR RESPONSE

1. What sin could keep you from the fulfillment of your desires?

2. How can you steer away from backsliding when God delays His response or says no to your requests?

Day

A IS FOR AUTHENTIC

When we struggle with unfulfilled desires, honesty is the best policy.

The beloved author of *Charlotte's Web,* E. B. White, said he was "not adverse to departing from reality" when writing for children, but was "against departing from the truth." [13]

When White wrote the fairy tale *The Trumpet of the Swan,* he read everything he could find about the trumpeter swan. He insisted "that however fantastical the tale, the behavior of the bird [in the story would be] authentic and violate nothing in the natural world of swans." [14]

Authentic. There's a frightening word. At least for writers immersed in ideas behind closed doors. It can be hours before we surface for air, turn doorknobs, and greet the world. Many times it's tempting to just breathe our solitude and forget coming out. It would be easier that way.

Easier than matching our words with actions. Simpler than working out relationships. More fantastical than trudging through an ordinary day. But a lot less authentic.

From woodwork to yellow documents, anything authentic denotes quality and originality. And sometimes that expectation from readers tempts me to turn off the word processor forever. Because authenticity is truth—and the truth can be costly.

I struggle with the truth when, occasionally, someone who's read my work wants to meet me. I panic. I wonder if I'm shorter, fatter, and older than she expected. I feel the pressure to utter pearls of wisdom when, really, I'd just been on my way to the bathroom, or angry with an employee, or taking a nap because the night before I'd procrastinated and then pulled an all-nighter to meet a deadline. I'm scared that this reader expects a mega woman when I'm very ordinary—and quite flawed.

It's the flawed part that scares me the most.

Even though we confess to our failures, some readers still view authors as almost-perfect specimens of humanity. And I don't really blame them. Authors with no flaws—and who always conquer—help readers believe that their lives can be seamless, too.

Except that's not authentic.

The truth is, life is messy and so are we. As I write this, I've relationships that need repairing, sins and addictions that keep returning, and hurts that need healing. Compared to most of my friends, who aren't stuck in front of a word processor every weekend, my life looks boring. And as soon as I write about overcoming a weakness, I can fall prey to it again.

With every project, I try to remind myself that it's my job to be a writer, just like it's someone else's calling to be a mother, a welder, a teacher, a lawyer. The best I can offer is to admit my mistakes and try not to repeat them. And to share how God forgives and walks through it with me.

Little by little, my writing challenges me to be authentic.

So does living with unfulfilled desires. What do I say to a young Christian who observes that God still hasn't answered my prayers? Or to an unbeliever who watches me sin and fail and get discouraged? Hopefully, an honest expression of my failings will ring more authentic than any spiritual platitude.

Come to think of it, isn't that what God asks His children to do, anyway? When we struggle with the failure of our desires, He says honesty is the best policy.

PERSONAL CHECKPOINT

1. Have you honestly expressed your disappointment to God? If not, why not?

2. Do you ever fear that unfulfilled desires will invalidate your spirituality or reputation with others? Explain.

GOD'S VIEWPOINT

A prayer for God's help in weakness:

> LORD, listen to me and answer me.
>   I am poor and helpless.
> Protect me, because I worship you.
>   My God, save me, your servant who trusts in you.
> Lord, have mercy on me,
>   because I have called to you all day.
> Give happiness to me, your servant,
>   because I give my life to you, Lord.
> Lord, you are kind and forgiving
>   and have great love for those who call to you.
> LORD, hear my prayer,
>   and listen when I ask for mercy.
> I call to you in times of trouble,
>   because you will answer me.
>
> Lord, there is no god like you
>   and no works like yours.
> Lord, all the nations you have made
>   will come and worship you.
>   They will honor you.
> You are great and you do miracles.
>   Only you are God.

> LORD, *teach me what you want me to do,*
> *and I will live by your truth.*
> *Teach me to respect you completely.*
> *Lord, my God, I will praise you with all my heart,*
> *and I will honor your name forever.*
> *You have great love for me.*
> *You have saved me from death.*
>
> *Lord, you are a God who shows mercy and is kind.*
> *You don't become angry quickly.*
> *You have great love and faithfulness.*
> *Turn to me and have mercy.*
> *Give me, your servant, strength.*
> *Save me, the son of your female servant.*
> *Show me a sign of your goodness.*
> *When my enemies look, they will be ashamed.*
> *You, LORD, have helped me and comforted me.*
> —*Psalm 86:1-13, 15-17*

YOUR RESPONSE

1. While living with unfulfilled desires, how can you stay authentic?

2. How can you be more honest with God?

Part Three

WHY NOT ME, LORD?

*Sorting out your expectant
beliefs and attitudes*

tars, not scars. Better or bitter?

*These phrases, along with a reminder that "all things
work together for good" often are offered by well-meaning Christians when you're in physical or emotional pain. They're given
as reminders that you have choices about your attitudes while
suffering. Even though the intentions are good, the phrases
can sound like worn-out clichés. Other people's expectations
can induce you to pretend as though you're handling pressure
points with grace and spirituality.*

*But looking good doesn't matter to God. He wants your
heart and soul to be healthy. He wants you to become more and
more like Jesus in your response to pain.*[15]

Janet Kobobel,
Where Is God When I Need Him Most?

I can only remember a few times when, in an effort to get my attention, God spoke to me in near-audible ways. Most often, He speaks to me through the Scriptures, through people with memorable words, through undeniable circumstances—and I'm usually comfortable with those approaches. But in these instances, God delivered zingers that bombarded my brain and rattled my thinking.

Once, while sitting in my car at the gas station, waiting for a fill-up, I watched a dirty, raggedy man hobble along the sidewalk. He looked intoxicated, and I sized him up as a loser.

Then a question startled my thoughts: *What makes you think you're any better than him?*

What? But I heard nothing more.

It didn't take long, though, to figure out the message. Life hadn't been going my way, and I'd blamed God for it. So with a few well-placed words, He challenged my demanding attitude: the belief that I was entitled to more than anyone else. God wanted me to know that He loves everyone equally and that my expectations needed an adjustment.

N ot long after that, I received my first free-lance writing assignment. Excited and nervous, I took the project seriously and wanted inspiration from God before beginning.

That weekend, I babysat a friend's dog and began work on the long-awaited assignment. However, I didn't have an idea for the piece, so I decided to pray about it first. I paced back and forth in the house, the dog alongside, asking God to bless my work and to give me a good idea.

Back and forth, back and forth, we paced. Then, with a flair for the dramatic, I dropped to the floor and prayed with my face down. The dog plopped to the floor beside me.

"Oh, God, please give me Your idea for writing this project," I prayed for the umpteenth time. The dog whined.

That's when I heard the answer.

It wasn't what I'd expected.

Get up and get to work, He said.

What? No praying and pleading?

Again, in a few startling words, God exposed my attitude. I'd been expecting Him to make up for toil on my part.

*W*hen life doesn't fulfill our desires, it's the attitude that fails first. And it's the attitude that directs how we pass through disappointment.

To this day, I still need to temper my demanding attitude and the tendency to expect God to accomplish what I could do myself. These attitudes surface most when I'm facing unmet expectations.

With attitudes, it seems there's no end to their need for adjustment. Fortunately, there's no end to God's grace and forgiveness, either.

PERSONAL CHECKPOINT

In Part Three, read about expectant beliefs and attitudes that could block the fulfillment of desires.

1. What negative attitudes might develop while waiting for the fulfillment of your desires?

2. Which attitude do you struggle with the most?

3. How could you adjust this attitude?

13

DARE TO BE MEDIOCRE

**Perfectionism keeps us on the
endless cycle of unmet expectations.**

y mother's complaints about me pivot on a childhood incident. When she recalls it, her usually gentle voice tinges with exasperation.

I don't blame her.

In the fourth grade, I fought with my friend Connie over who was the smartest between us. I claimed the most intelligence; so did she. We finally decided that whoever earned the best grades that school year would win our argument.

The results were a grade-school teacher's dream. I diligently completed my homework, studied hard for tests, and earned straight A's every quarter. My parents delighted in it. Connie—who got a couple of B grades—conceded to my achievement. And I got depressed.

According to my mother, I wanted to be better than perfect. She reasoned with me, but I still longed for the impossible. My perfectionism has bothered her ever since.

*F*unny thing, this quest for perfection. It can serve you well; it can do you in. The trick is to stop fussing before you cross the line from excellence to outrageousness. Or before you demoralize yourself or someone else.

For example, when an art director at work asked my opinion of a page design, I gave my advice and then began critiquing other details on the layout—before he was finished with it. Fortunately, I caught myself and exited without driving him crazy. Walking back to my office, I mentally chanted, *Setting a standard for quality is good; nit-picking people toward delirium is not.*

Franklin D. Roosevelt once said that perfectionism may obstruct the paths to international peace.[16] Most of us, however, feel more concerned about how it blocks the inner roadways of our souls. Untamed, perfectionism can rob our tranquility and mire us in misery.

A management consultant put it this way: "Nothing gives a sense of failure so often as an overdeveloped sense of perfection. This leads a person to set impossible standards for himself. Perfectionism is good in a moderate dose, but overdeveloped, it results in feelings of guilt over failures when, by ordinary standards or even extra-high standards, a [person] would be judged a success."[17]

Most of us aren't as unrealistic as a fourth-grader who's discontented with perfect grades. But these days, I know few women who're contented with their lives. Unless we receive or achieve 100 percent of our desires, we're disappointed and feel like failures. We constantly view the cup as half empty rather than half full.

We're suffering from the disease of perfectionism, and it sounds like this:

"I won't be happy unless *all* of my children come home for the Christmas holidays."

"I finally got Sandy to attend church with me. Now, if she'd only go to Sunday school."

"No job will be good enough until I'm president of my own company."

"I'd enjoy this beautiful house if my husband would be here more often."

In her book, *Perfect Women*, Colette Dowling described the plague of perfectionism that's ravaging today's women.

"A belief in the possibility of perfecting ourselves is the chief illusion seducing women today," she wrote, and for several chapters, Colette traced how this malady exudes from feelings of inferiority. [18] We secretly and mistakenly believe that, if we can get life *exactly* the way we want it, then we'll be happy with ourselves.

*T*he obvious but overlooked hole in our thinking rests on the fact we live in an imperfect world. Sin robbed us of God's ideal, and as long as we're on earth, we're destined to live with imperfection. Still, that doesn't mean we can't be content—or that we can't tame perfectionism. Through the Cross, God provided a way to reckon with our imperfect selves.

Reduced to its roots, perfectionism becomes a spiritual dilemma. Will we accept that we live in an imperfect world? Will we embrace our imperfections—and the imperfections of others—but rejoice that through Christ's redemption we're acceptable in God's eyes? Will we allow ourselves to be content, despite the fact that an imperfect world will never fulfill all of our expectations?

These questions take a lifetime to answer wholeheartedly. But when our souls gradually answer yes, we begin to taste life at its best.

My friend Liz, who's struggled against the desire to be perfect, coined a slogan to help herself be more contented. "I call it 'Dare to Be Mediocre,'" she laughed and described how, with this humorous approach, she gave herself permission to accept life and to stop the relentless pursuit of perfectionism. Observing her for the last few years, I'd add that she even dared to be happy, despite unfulfilled expectations.

Content and happy? I can hear God saying, "I dare you."

PERSONAL CHECKPOINT

1. Are you perfectionistic about your unfulfilled desires? If so, how?

2. Is feeling content with your life an appealing idea to you? Why, or why not?

GOD'S VIEWPOINT

Paul encourages the Philippians to be content:

Be full of joy in the Lord always. I will say again, be full of joy.
Let everyone see that you are gentle and kind. The Lord is coming
soon. Do not worry about anything, but pray and ask God for everything
you need, always giving thanks. And God's peace, which is so great we
cannot understand it, will keep your hearts and minds in Christ Jesus.

Brothers and sisters, think about the things that are good and wor-
thy of praise. Think about the things that are true and honorable and
right and pure and beautiful and respected. Do what you have learned
and received from me, what I told you, and what you saw me do. And the
God who gives peace will be with you.

I am very happy in the Lord that you have shown your care for me
again. You continued to care about me, but there was no way for you to
show it. I am not telling you this because I need anything. I have learned
to be satisfied with the things I have and with everything that happens. I
know how to live when I am poor, and I know how to live when I have
plenty. I have learned the secret of being happy at any time in everything
that happens, when I have enough to eat and when I go hungry, when I
have more than I need and when I do not have enough. I can do all things
through Christ, because he gives me strength.
—Philippians 4:4-13

YOUR RESPONSE

1. How could you become contented with life now, despite unmet expectations?

2. How can you differentiate between contentment and laziness?

THE ART OF
SELF-SABOTAGE

Laziness destroys our dreams.

Nothing nosedives me faster than trying on clothes in a department store. It's the singular act that makes me face that I'm overweight.

I can manage rifling through the larger-than-before sizes—even keep the sales lady from entering the dressing room while I'm changing—but I wilt in front of those mirrors that reveal my lumps in three ways instead of one.

Each shopping trip, I resolve to take action against my weighty condition. And I have. I've shopped through the mail, purchased styles that cover up fat, and quit weighing myself. I've sought consolation in overweight friends and blamed the people at work who keep candy jars on their desks. I've tried lots of things—except the action I need most.

Now facing the truth and starting a diet sounds simple, but it's not. In his best-selling book, *The Road Less Traveled*, psychotherapist M. Scott Peck wrote: "The difficulty we have in accepting the responsibility for our behavior lies in the desire to avoid the pain of the consequences of that behavior . . . but attempting to avoid the pain of responsibility, millions and billions daily attempt to escape from freedom." [19]

As a result, we practice self-sabotage and become our own worst enemy.

*W*hy do we blockade the thing that we most desire? It takes work to make dreams come true, and our laziness fears the exertion it takes to follow those desires, especially if the pursuit involves changing ourselves. In a quirky way, we fear success because new levels of achievement carry greater amounts of responsibility.

Now we might protest, "I'm not lazy! I'm the busiest person I know; I want to be a success." But laziness gnaws at the schedules of some of the most disciplined. It's why they get organized—and why we pack our days with activities and attend time-management workshops.

A woman whose accomplishments I admire once confided, "If I don't overload my schedule with activities, I know that I'll move toward inertia. I am very lazy, so I impose busyness on myself to keep going."

Another complained, "When my schedule is busiest, my laziness fights back in grand style. Sometimes, I feel as though I'm pushing a huge stone up a hill, and it's constantly threatening to roll back and crush me."

Peck called laziness the original sin, and claimed it often expresses itself in fear. He explained: "No matter how energetic, ambitious, or even wise we may be, if we truly look into ourselves we will find laziness lurking at some level. It is the force of entropy within us, pushing us down and holding us all back from our spiritual evolution." [20] And holding us back from our deep desires.

*R*eleasing ourselves from laziness begins with admitting the truth. Admitting the truth about ourselves is a spiritual act, the catalyst for release from what binds us. Admitting the truth is the foundation for change. It is a protective wall that our sin nature fights against. It is the door to freedom and the fulfillment of our desires.

Still, after admitting the truth, we must keep walking in it to push past self-sabotage; to ignite the inertia that holds us back; to unleash the dreams trapped within us. For each of us, this walk of truth looks different, but at the core, we recognize the need for God to bring us out of the darkness (or out of the dressing room) and into the light.

When we are our own worst enemy, He is the lover of our souls. And the more we know and depend on His love, the less we will fear ourselves and our dreams.

PERSONAL CHECKPOINT

1. Do you sabotage your dreams? If so, how?

2. Do you fight a laziness that holds you back?

GOD'S VIEWPOINT

How the Lord responds to our weaknesses:

> My whole being, praise the LORD;
>   all my being, praise his holy name.
> My whole being, praise the LORD
>   and do not forget all his kindnesses.
> He forgives all my sins
>   and heals all my diseases.
> He saves my life from the grave
>   and loads me with love and mercy.
> He satisfies me with good things
>   and makes me young again, like the eagle.
>
> The LORD does what is right and fair
>   for all who are wronged by others.
> He showed his ways to Moses
>   and his deeds to the people of Israel.
> The LORD shows mercy and is kind.

He does not become angry quickly, and he has great love.
He will not always accuse us,
  and he will not be angry forever.
He has not punished us as our sins should be punished;
  he has not repaid us for the evil we have done.
As high as the sky is above the earth,
  so great is his love for those who respect him.
He has taken our sins away from us
  as far as the east is from west.
The LORD has mercy on those who respect him,
  as a father has mercy on his children.
He knows how we were made;
  he remembers that we are dust.

It is good to sing praises to our God;
  it is good and pleasant to praise him.
The LORD rebuilds Jerusalem;
  he brings back the captured Israelites.
He heals the brokenhearted
  and bandages their wounds.
He counts the stars
  and names each one.
Our Lord is great and very powerful.
  There is no limit to what he knows.
                              —*Psalm 103:1-14; 147:1b-5*

YOUR RESPONSE

1. How could admitting the truth help fulfill your desires?

2. How can you depend more on God's love?

THE COST OF COMPARISONS

**Comparing our circumstances with others
can lead to isolation and spiritual neglect.**

*I*t's been a nerve-racking week. Each new day brought more worries about friends.

Monday morning. A letter arrived from Donna, who's in Mexico with her husband. He's getting treatments for cancer that recurred after a ten-year remission. Unless God performs a miracle, these could be his final days.

Monday afternoon. Frances from Atlanta called to say her daughter Jessica tested positive for HIV. Jessica contracted the virus from the intravenous use of cocaine.

Monday evening. I received a postcard from Amanda, a friend from my hometown. She wrote: *I wanted to give you my new address as John [her husband] and I are separating . . . maybe someday it will work.*

Tuesday evening. From suburban Chicago, Cindy's husband called to announce that she delivered her second child. (Good news!) The labor only lasted for thirty minutes. (Is that really possible?) A girl.

Later Tuesday evening. I discovered that my longtime friend Christie has suffered in labor all day, trying to deliver a baby who could die if certain complications occur.

Wednesday. Christie and her still undelivered baby developed fevers. After two days of hard labor, she finally birthed a daughter whom nurses ushered into intensive care.

I ate dinner with a local friend who's contemplating divorce from a man she can't tolerate anymore.

Thursday. DeeAnne from Dallas called to describe how, two months ago, her five-year-old son was hit in the head by a car. His brain swelled, but remarkably, he recovered without lasting damage.

Friday. I called my mother and learned that Sandy's fourteen-year-old son has only two months to live. Sandy and I were best friends in junior high.

*A*fter a week like that, I feel helplessly out of control. Since most of these friends live out-of-state, there's not much I can do to help them. So I worry—and wonder if God still rules the universe.

I wonder why one mother's son lies dying while another mother's son miraculously lives. Why one friend labored in childbirth for a half-hour while, on the same day, another friend's birthing process turned horrific. Why some women find wedded bliss while others suffer in marriages from hell.

Strangely, none of these women know each other. I am the only common link to their emergencies. So I also wonder—if these women knew one another—whether they'd find comfort or confusion in the different ways God responded to their pain. Whether they'd compare their tragedies and wallow in self-pity or lock arms and support one another. Whether they'd feel perplexed and frustrated with life's inconsistencies, as I did last week, or if they'd respond with peace and strength.

To be honest, I'm relieved that I'll never find out. They're a fabulous group of women, but I know the heart turns self-protective when it's disappointed.

I have seen it happen to friends. I've done it myself. When one woman receives what another woman wants, their relationship suffers. The woman who's left with unfulfilled desires thinks, *Why did she get what she wanted? She's no better than I am!* She wants sympathy. The woman who's obtained her dreams doesn't face her friend's pain. She wants to enjoy herself. Consequently, the women avoid each other, and if the friendship doesn't end, it's never the same again.

It's also a time when both women can neglect God out of bitterness or arrogance.

Yet I've felt the warmth and smelled the sweetness when two women, with drastically different circumstances, let the unfulfilled desires between them bind their souls together. When they ask questions and listen. When they answer graciously, yet honestly. When they decide nothing is worth breaking up sisterhood. When they live out Christ's admonition to love our neighbors as ourselves.

It's a tough transition. But the aftermath yields the depth of relationship we're constantly searching for. And it's how nonbelievers discover God lovingly at work in the world.

PERSONAL CHECKPOINT

1. With whom are you tempted to compare your circumstances? Why?

2. What is the cost of making these comparisons?

GOD'S VIEWPOINT

John writes about loving one another:

Dear friends, we should love each other, because love comes from God. Everyone who loves has become God's child and knows God. Whoever does not love does not know God, because God is love. This is how God showed his love to us: He sent his one and only Son into the world so that we could have life through him. This is what real love is: It is not our love for God; it is God's love for us in sending his Son to be the way to take away our sins.

Dear friends, if God loved us that much we also should love each other. No one has ever seen God, but if we love each other, God lives in us, and his love is made perfect in us.

We know that we live in God and he lives in us, because he gave us his Spirit. We have seen and can testify that the Father sent his Son to be the Savior of the world. Whoever confesses that Jesus is the Son of God has God living inside, and that person lives in God. And so we know the love that God has for us, and we trust that love.

God is love. Those who live in love live in God, and God lives in them. This is how love is made perfect in us: that we can be without fear on the day God judges us, because in this world we are like him.

We love because God first loved us. If people say, "I love God," but hate their brothers or sisters, they are liars. Those who do not love their brothers and sisters, whom they have seen, cannot love God, whom they have never seen. And God gave us this command: Those who love God must also love their brothers and sisters.

—1 John 4:7-17, 19-21

YOUR RESPONSE

1. How can you truly love those whose lives seem better than yours?

2. What is the cost of loving this way?

Day 16

HOW DO YOU MEASURE MORE?

Sometimes unfulfilled expectations
point to a relentless desire for more.

n conversations with a trusted friend, the actress Greta Garbo described her desire to become a legend. She said:

> As far back as I can remember in my memory, I have always wanted to be like Sarah Bernhardt. I even tried to imitate her acting, but my Shakespeare used to come out too realistic, and the theatrical possibilities for me in Stockholm were rather limited.
>
> It was my meeting with Mauritz Stiller [Moje] so early in life that put me on the film road. . . . I was fortunate to meet and to receive love and help from a man like Moje. I was lucky that he handpicked me, but I was also lucky that I had the capacity to learn quickly from him and work hard.
>
> I'm not sure, honestly speaking, that other people helped me that much, because I always despised them. I always felt that they were not necessary for the success that I had achieved and secured more permanently

than anyone else in the film industry, save perhaps Chaplin.

I despise people even more today, because I don't need them to build my fame, and I don't need them in my daily life. I believe—perhaps illogically—that if I bring people closer to myself, they may discover my real character and through their maneuverings and gossiping I might lose my legend.

My legend is everything to me now. I would not sell it for life, happiness, or anyone, including my sister, my father, or Moje. As a matter of fact, I would even sacrifice my own life so as not to jeopardize it. [21]

Garbo's insatiable desire for fame eventually compelled her to withdraw from society when her film reviews turned sour. If she couldn't have more fame through movies, she carefully calculated more fame through her mysterious aloofness. Sadly, in her old age, this mystique turned her into a recluse.

*G*reta grew extreme in her request for more, but quite honestly, I'm afraid I'm getting a bit "Garboesque" about some of my expectations. Writing a book consumes me, and before I've finished this manuscript, I'm already wondering whether a publisher will allow me to write another one. For years, I've felt it's the next project that will be my best—as long as someone will give me another chance to publish.

It's worse with my house. I bought a new family room couch, but the area won't look right until I recover a chair to match it. Then the chair will need pillows. In the meantime, I bought an entertainment center. After that, the room called for a new rug to pull it all together. Now the room looks lopsided and needs a bookshelf to balance it off. And, of course, no decor is finished without paintings and other accessories.

Repeated throughout a nine-room house, I'm on a constant quest for "just one more thing" to make the place look good. With my resources, decorating the house will become a several-year project. But already, I'm beginning to wonder if I'll ever be satisfied with the results—that maybe I've unleashed an unquenchable desire for more.

I also wonder if the book and house have become so paramount, that I'm dwindling important relationships.

*W*hen it comes to fulfilling our desires, how can we tell whether we're really on a quest for more, more, more? It's probably our first clue when the desire becomes immeasurable or insatiable or both. Those descriptors belong to God, and when we're measuring our unfulfilled expectations, we need His help to determine what their size and limit should be.

PERSONAL CHECKPOINT

1. Are any of your unfulfilled expectations built on a desire to acquire more?

2. What motivates you to acquire more?

GOD'S VIEWPOINT

Jesus cautions against the desire to have more:

Be careful and guard against all kinds of greed. Life is not measured by how much one owns.

. . . There was a rich man who had some land, which grew a good crop. He thought to himself, "What will I do? I have no place to keep all my crops." Then he said, "This is what I will do: I will tear down my barns and build bigger ones, and there I will store all my grain and other goods. Then I can say to myself, 'I have enough good things stored to last for many years. Rest, eat, drink, and enjoy life!'"

But God said to him, "Foolish man! Tonight your life will be taken from you. So who will get those things you have prepared for yourself?"

This is how it will be for those who store up things for themselves and are not rich toward God.

Don't fear, little flock, because your Father wants to give you the kingdom. Sell your possessions and give to the poor. Get for yourselves purses that will not wear out, the treasure in heaven that never runs out, where thieves can't steal and moths can't destroy. Your heart will be where your treasure is.

—Luke 12:15-21, 32-34

Your Response

1. What do your unmet expectations reveal about where your "treasure" is?

2. How can you become rich toward God instead of things?

REAL WOMEN DON'T DO INSTANT GARDENS

***Sometimes God delays our desires so
He can change what's thorny about us.***

oday, I set stiff goals for writing more entries in this book. So naturally, I wound up puttering in my flower gardens. (A prolific author once told me he works on five books at a time so he can always procrastinate on four!) But casting aside a writer's bent toward delaying her work, what draws me to the flower beds?

I'm new to the gardening life, but along with dirt diggers through the ages, I'm already espousing the joys of getting close to nature and respecting its rhythms. I suspect it's a throwback to Eden, when the Creator assigned gardening tasks to Adam and Eve, and on my more philosophical days, I think of myself as participating in an ancient ritual of tending the earth on God's behalf. My mind floats to my mother, grandmother, and multitudes of women before them who followed their instincts to create and nurture—and fell captive to the mystical sights and smells of the flower garden.

These romantic musings, however, don't negate the fact that gardening requires hard work. At the job, I use the buzz words "labor intensive" to describe time-consuming projects. But in my yard, I know it's just a lot of bending, stooping, pulling, pushing, hauling, digging, clipping and pinching that makes a garden grow. And if I'm into instant gratification, this isn't the place to be.

*F*or most of my life, I've felt lured by the siren of instant gratification. My sister insists that, as a newborn, I popped out of the womb wanting things my way, right away. I resist her description of me as the spoiled, youngest child. Yet I know that, personally and professionally, I've chosen short-term activities and writing projects that provide instant gratification for my efforts. I recognize that this sister speaks with a kernel of truth.

So gardening marks a transition of outlook and character for me. Planting a new bed of bulbs last fall meant waiting out the cold months until, a few weeks ago, tulips and daffodils peeked from the ground. Yet this morning, when neighbors strolled by and complimented the profusion of red and yellow, I calmly said "thank you" instead of describing my hard work or explaining that, although the rest of the yard looks bare, I'm preparing it for future glories.

These strollers won't watch me prune the rosebushes, till and enrich the flower-bed soil, pore through seed catalogs, map out garden plans, plant summer bulbs, transplant stray daylilies, scour the local nurseries for equipment, tend to a compost, plant the lilac bushes, attack the dandelions, spend too much money on plantings, keep the cat from eating the herbs, or spray, fertilize, and water it all. But they will notice and admire the eventual results: a creative expression of beauty.

In the end, it's the hope of beauty that sustains me through the dormant and preparatory months when I'm either cutting things back or burying them in the ground and when dirty work yields no perceptible rewards except sore muscles and an aching back. Even I—the writer of all things short—have accepted that, in the garden, there's no instant anything.

I have also fallen to another labored habit that gardeners annoy their friends with: talking about what we've learned from the garden (after first describing in detail everything we *did* in the garden). So, of course, there's a spiritual application midst these ramblings. The idea isn't original, but as I've worked in the yard, I've thought of how gardening principles relate to the fulfillment of my desires.

Throughout nature, there's a cyclical pattern of dying to eventually spring back with new life. In the fall, I cut down, cover up, and abandon the flower beds. Looking out my kitchen window in December, it seems doubtful that they'll ever bloom again. Yet the same view during July will crowd with color, if I exercise faith and perseverance during the months between.

Jesus said that unless a grain of wheat falls to the ground and dies, it will never yield a harvest (John 12:24). So it's been with my unmet expectations. Before fulfilling my desires, God often cuts down those dreams and buries them in a character development process that feels like death. Then later, when I'm content to live without them, He resurrects those desires and hands them to me. They're more beautiful and bountiful than I'd imagined, and I realize they're a product of the dormant and difficult times of a winter past.

Strangely enough, friends and family members don't notice my fulfilled desires as much as they point out the changes in me. I haven't yet become an object of beauty. (Unfortunately, character shaping requires a lifetime rather than just four seasons.) But I'm encouraged to know that, if I'm faithful, God will express His creativity through someone as thorny as me.

PERSONAL CHECKPOINT

1. In regard to your unmet expectations, what season of the year are you in? Why?

2. What character building might God be accomplishing in you during this season?

GOD'S VIEWPOINT

More admonitions from the psalmist:

> *Trust the LORD and do good.*
> *Live in the land and feed on truth.*

Enjoy serving the Lord,
  and he will give you what you want.
Depend on the Lord;
  trust him, and he will take care of you.
Then your goodness will shine like the sun,
  and your fairness like the noonday sun.

When a person's steps follow the Lord,
  God is pleased with his ways.
If he stumbles, he will not fall,
  because the Lord holds his hand.

I was young, and now I am old,
  but I have never seen good people left helpless
  or their children begging for food.
Good people always lend freely to others,
  and their children are a blessing.

Stop doing evil and do good,
  so you will live forever.
The Lord loves justice
  and will not leave those who worship him.

Wait for the Lord's help
  and follow him.
He will honor you and give you the land.
                              —Psalm 37:3-6, 23-28a, 34b

Your Response

1. How can you depend on God during the dormant and difficult times?

2. How can you wait for the Lord?

DYING TO PLEASE

***Trying to appease people can keep us
from pursuing our God-given desires.***

etween the years 620 and 560 B.C., an ex-slave arrived in
the court of Croesus, the last of the kings of Lydia in Asia
Minor. Named Aesop, this freedman gained fame and respect as a
narrator of fables about animals.

Despite the changes of twenty-five centuries, Aesop's fables
still thrive and teach us lessons today. For example, read the story
of "The Miller, His Son, and Their Donkey."

> A miller and his son were driving their donkey to a
> neighboring fair to sell him. They had not gone far
> when they met a group of girls returning from town,
> laughing and talking together.
>
> "Look, there!" cried one of them. "Did you ever
> see such fools, to be trudging along the road on foot,
> when they ought to be riding!"
>
> So the man put the boy on the donkey, and they
> went on their way. Presently, they came up to a group
> of old men in earnest debate.

"There!" said one of them. "That proves exactly what I was saying. No one pays any respect to old age in these days. Look at that idle young rogue riding, while his poor old father has to walk. Get down, you lazy lout, and let the old man rest his weary limbs."

The miller made his son dismount and got on the donkey's back in his place. And in this manner, they proceeded along the way until they met a company of women and children.

"Why, shame on you, lazybones!" they cried. "How can you ride while that poor little lad can hardly keep up with you?" The good miller, wishing to please, took up his son to sit behind him.

But just as they reached the edge of the village, a townsman called out to them: "I have a good mind to report you to the authorities for overloading that poor beast so shamelessly. You big, hulking fellows should better be able to carry that donkey than the other way around."

So, sighing, the miller and his son tied the beast's legs together, and with a pole across their shoulders, carried the donkey over the bridge that led to the town. This was such an entertaining sight to the towns-folk that crowds came out to laugh at it.

The poor animal, frightened by the uproar, began to struggle to free himself. In the midst of the turmoil, the ass slipped off the pole and over the rail of the bridge, into the water and was drowned.

Application: Try to please all and you end by pleasing none. [22]

*I*t's still true. When we try to please too many people, we wind up pleasing no one. Not even ourselves—and especially not God. People pleasing can blur His unique vision for us and leave us with mounds of unmet dreams and expectations.

Women especially entrench themselves in people pleasing. Husbands, children, employers, extended family, and friends can demand so much that we lose sight of God's vision for us. We become slaves to too many masters.

"No one can serve two masters," said Jesus. "The person will hate one master and love the other, or will follow one master and refuse to follow the other" (Mathew 6:24). We can end up despising ourselves, too, if we never follow the quiet voice within us.

I'm not suggesting that we stop loving and serving people, but that we put them into proper perspective to follow God's personal call to us. When we're frustrated about living with unfulfilled desires, it helps to ask, "Am I so busy pleasing others that I'm not fulfilling God's purpose for me?"

The answer could be surprising and life changing.

PERSONAL CHECKPOINT

1. Are you trying to please too many people and missing your heart's desires? How do you feel about this?

2. What tempts you toward people pleasing?

GOD'S VIEWPOINT

Christ's startling words about people pleasing:

All those who stand before others and say they believe in me, I will say before my Father in heaven that they belong to me. But all who stand before others and say they do not believe in me, I will say before my Father in heaven that they do not belong to me.

Don't think that I came to bring peace to the earth. I did not come to bring peace, but a sword. I have come so that
    "a son will be against his father,
      a daughter will be against her mother,
    a daughter-in-law will be against her mother-in-law.
      A person's enemies will be members of his own family."
Those who love their father or mother more than they love me are not worthy to be my followers. Those who love their son or daughter more than they love me are not worthy to be my followers. Whoever is not willing to carry the cross and follow me is not worthy of me. Those who try to hold on to their lives will give up true life. Those who give up their lives for me will

hold on to true life. Whoever accepts you also accepts me, and whoever accepts me also accepts the One who sent me. Whoever meets a prophet and accepts him will receive the reward of a prophet. And whoever accepts a good person because that person is good will receive the reward of a good person. Those who give one of these little ones a cup of cold water because they are my followers will truly get their reward.

—Matthew 10:32-42

YOUR RESPONSE

1. In your life, what will it mean to please God more than people?

2. Have you neglected fulfilling any of God's desires for you? If so, how can you begin to fulfill them?

Part Four

LIVING IN
THE NOW

Accepting your life, one day at a time

he son asked, What is the secret of continued endurance?

His Father answered, It is found in seeing Him who is invisible. It is found in looking at the joy that is set before thee. It is found in considering Him who endured.

It is found in taking for thine own the words of one who was tempted to wax faint, "In the day when I cried Thou answeredst me, and strengthenedst me with strength in my soul." It is found in staking thine all upon the lightest word of the Lord, thy Redeemer. It is found in loyalty. It is found in love. [23]

Amy Carmichael,
His thoughts said . . . His Father said . . .

*I*n my early twenties, I weathered a difficult roommate arrangement. One of my resentments toward Becky festered on her hope-chest items stuffed in odd crannies around our rambling, old apartment.

For instance, every time she opened the living-room closet and inadvertently displayed an unused Tupperware set crammed on the top shelf, I sighed.

"I want to save them for marriage," she'd explained. So we used and broke my dishes and appliances. And while Becky hoped for nuptial bliss, I fantasized about confiscating her plastic containers for our next round of leftovers.

Becky's wait-for-later outlook bugged me at other points, too. When I needed to clean behind our refrigerator, I asked her to help pull the appliance away from a kitchen wall.

"Oh, no," she protested. "We should wait for a man to do that."

Since men are generally physically stronger than women, her comment sounded logical. But we didn't have access to a male who could help, and the job could have been easily accomplished by the two of us. After explaining these facts to Becky, she still demurred. So I shoved out the refrigerator by myself.

Eventually, Becky and I forgave our differences and stayed friends. And if I'd listened to her protestations, I probably wouldn't suffer with back problems today. But I still believe that young, single women should collect domestic goods for an apartment instead of a hope chest, because they don't know how long the interval between school and marriage will exist, and gaining independence doesn't mean losing femininity or the hope for marriage.

*M*y anger toward Becky probably foretold the school-marriage gap that never closed for me. And through the years, I've wrestled with frustration while observing women—including myself—who don't face singleness realistically. We totter between two types: women who forget the future and don't make career or financial plans, or others who worry so much about getting married that they don't enjoy today. Both types concede to the Cinderella complex, our belief that men will rescue and take care of us.

This rescue mentality, however, doesn't contain itself within the boundaries of men and marriage. Married women suffer from it, too. When life doesn't meet our expectations, it's easier to fantasize about someone solving the problem for us rather than facing reality and adjusting to it . . . or to deny the problem altogether rather than changing what needs to be fixed. Something deep within us resists the demise of our dreams.

Ironically, it's nearly impossible to obtain those dreams until we reckon with today's realities. The same inner fortitude that helps us realistically and contentedly walk through each day also infuses us with the hope and courage to change and affect the future. And in the spiritual realm, God may delay miracles until we've accepted His lordship over the daily and the mundane.

Jesus told us to forget about tomorrow's worries. That begins with taking care of ourselves today.

PERSONAL CHECKPOINT

While reading Part Four, think of the ways you can accept today's realities while waiting for tomorrow's dreams.

1. Do you harbor a rescue mentality toward your unfulfilled expectations?

2. What's difficult about accepting your life today?

3. What keeps you from facing today's realities?

TRUTH OR CONSEQUENCES

***Bitterness about our lives today
creates problems for tomorrow.***

ears before women employed themselves outside the home, Maggie worked as a lawyer and loved it. A few years into her career, she married a handsome young architect and, within months, got pregnant. Maggie decided to stay home with her daughter, but more because of family expectations than her own desires. She planned a return to practice when her daughter entered school.

Instead, Maggie gave birth to another daughter. And another. Maggie hadn't planned on these second and third babies, and she imagined the years stretching before her with nothing but mounds of dirty diapers in sight. She loved her daughters, but sometimes she felt depressed and annoyed by their intrusion on her professional work.

Then the unthinkable happened. Her husband, full of promise for a brilliant career, decided to quit his job and train for the pastorate. In those days, a pastor's wife didn't work outside the parsonage, except to engage in church activities. Maggie visualized her law practice in flames.

Despite her impassioned protests, Maggie's husband packed up his family to attend seminary and later took them to several small churches around the country. He loved his work and the congregations admired him. Maggie, with her dead dreams, felt trapped and grew bitter.

At first she stuffed the disappointment within her, but as the years passed, Maggie began poisoning relationships with it. She regularly criticized church members and particularly the women, whom she considered stupid and unambitious. She railed at her husband and picked at her daughters with a persistent perfectionism.

Beneath it all, I believe Maggie hated herself for losing her dreams, for becoming the woman she didn't want to be, for her abject unhappiness. She wouldn't accept the demise of her career and, consequently, refused to enjoy life. She practiced denial in one of its ugliest forms: the kind that torpedoes everyone within shooting range.

More years passed and Maggie and her husband eventually exited the ministry. Their church and children had grown troubled and, as a surprise to few people, Maggie had descended into deep despair. Unfortunately, leaving the pastorate didn't improve Maggie's outlook, and she suffered rounds of doctors and medication and hospitalization in an attempt to revive her soul.

Eventually, Maggie died, only in her forties, in a hospital for the mentally disturbed. Some say she committed suicide.

I do not relay this story to criticize Maggie or her husband or her family. In fact, I've often wondered if, given the same circumstances, I'd behave much worse than Maggie. Losing our dreams can traumatize us.

On the other hand, refusing to accept our lives creates repugnant circumstances. We can descend into a bitterness so blinding that we can't consider creative options or recognize a "second chance" when it arrives. We're too busy pitying ourselves.

We let the truth strangle us when Jesus said the truth can set us free to live productively (John 8:31).

Avoiding the bitter consequences of dead dreams means releasing our lives to God each day. Bit by bit, our denial tears us down and, little by little, His truth builds us up.

When the road splits into two paths, it's better to follow the pain of truth than the numbness of denial. The truth can lead to life and joy. Denial leads to pain and death. The path we choose will make all the difference.

PERSONAL CHECKPOINT

1. Have you recognized the truth about your life today? Explain.

2. Do you harbor any bitterness about this reality?

GOD'S VIEWPOINT

Jesus told the Jews:

"If you continue to obey my teaching, you are truly my followers. Then you will know the truth, and the truth will make you free."

They answered, "We are Abraham's children, and we have never been anyone's slaves. So why do you say we will be free?"

Jesus answered, "I tell you the truth, everyone who lives in sin is a slave to sin. A slave does not stay with a family forever, but a son belongs to the family forever. So if the Son makes you free, you will be truly free. I know you are Abraham's children, but you want to kill me because you don't accept my teaching. I am telling you what my Father has shown me, but you do what your father has told you."

They answered, "Our father is Abraham."

Jesus said, "If you were really Abraham's children, you would do the things Abraham did. I am a man who has told you the truth which I heard from God, but you are trying to kill me. Abraham did nothing like that. So you are doing the things your own father did."

But they said, "We are not like children who never knew who their father was. God is our Father; he is the only Father we have."

Jesus said to them, "If God were really your Father, you would love me, because I came from God and now I am here. I did not come by my own authority; God sent me. You don't understand what I say, because you cannot accept my teaching. You belong to your father the devil, and you want to do what he wants. He was a murderer from the beginning

and was against the truth, because there is no truth in him. When he tells a lie, he shows what he is really like, because he is a liar and the father of lies. But because I speak the truth, you don't believe me. Can any of you prove that I am guilty of sin? If I am telling the truth, why don't you believe me? The person who belongs to God accepts what God says. But you don't accept what God says, because you don't belong to God."
                                                          —John 8:31-47

YOUR RESPONSE

1. How could Satan be keeping you from the truth?

2. What daily descents into denial might you need to overcome?

THE PRACTICE OF FAITH

Spiritual discipline builds tenacity for times of uncertainty.

*I*n her last year of life, the celebrated dancer Martha Graham published *Blood Memory*, an autobiographical account of her life and dance philosophy. The opening paragraphs described her daily regime of practice and underscored a principle of life.

Martha wrote:

> I am a dancer.
>
> I believe that we learn by practice. Whether it means to learn to dance by practicing dancing or to learn to live by practicing living, the principles are the same. In each it is the performance of a dedicated precise set of acts, physical or intellectual, from which comes the shape of achievement, a sense of one's being, a satisfaction of spirit. One becomes in some area an athlete of God.
>
> To practice means to perform, in the face of all obstacles, some act of vision, of faith, of desire. Practice is a means of inviting the perfection desired.

I think the reason dance has held such an ageless magic for the world is that it has been the symbol of the performance of living. Even as I write, time has begun to make today yesterday—the past. The most brilliant scientific discoveries will in time change and perhaps grow obsolete, as new scientific manifestations emerge. But art is eternal, for it reveals the inner landscape, which is the soul of man.

Many times I hear the phrase "the dance of life." It is an expression that touches me deeply, for the instrument through which the dance speaks is also the instrument through which life is lived—the human body. . . .

Dancing appears glamorous, easy, delightful. But the path to the paradise of the achievement is not easier than any other. There is fatigue so great that the body cries, even in its sleep. There are times of complete frustration, there are daily small deaths. Then I need all the comfort that practice has stored in my memory, a tenacity of faith. [24]

*W*hen dancing grew difficult, Martha drew on the discipline learned in daily practice.

It's an apt metaphor for our spiritual lives. The daily practice of faith—of deliberately walking with God—develops our strength for passing through uncertain and difficult times. It strengthens our spiritual muscles, so when they're stretched, we don't snap under the pressure.

An indelible example of this discipline shines through my friend Madalene. Not long ago, her husband died from cancer. And though she's grieving, there's a peace permeating her spirit.

At first, I feared Madalene might be in denial. But as I've watched her pass through this valley, I've changed my mind. She's walked closely with God for many years, and the daily practice of His presence has produced a strength she relies on now.

Madalene says it's the result of daily choices. "When Harlan first became ill, I chose to practice thanking God for everything and believing that all things work together for good," she explained to me at lunch one day. "That sustains me during the grief."

Now in her sixties, Madalene didn't start to obey God's Word when death approached her home. She'd been choosing the right way for years—and that discipline guides her through the shadowlands. Unfortunately, I'm unaccustomed to people walking this close to God, and I almost mistook the Holy Spirit's work for a possible dysfunction.

After our lunch together, I returned home inspired by my friend's example—and chastised that I'd fallen into the habit of calling on God only when I need Him, rather than communicating with Him as a friend every day. When my desires remain unfulfilled and I pass through the valley of disappointment, I need the "tenacity of faith" that only practice can develop within me.

Personal Checkpoint

1. Do you need to develop the discipline of walking with God every day?

2. How can this discipline comfort you while living with unfulfilled desires?

God's Viewpoint

A song of trust in God:

> *The Lord is my light and the one who saves me.*
> *I fear no one.*
> *The Lord protects my life;*
> *I am afraid of no one.*
> *Evil people may try to destroy my body.*
> *My enemies and those who hate me attack me,*
> *but they are overwhelmed and defeated.*
> *If an army surrounds me,*
> *I will not be afraid.*
> *If war breaks out,*
> *I will trust the Lord.*

I ask only one thing from the LORD.
  This is what I want:
Let me live in the LORD's house
  all my life.
Let me see the LORD's beauty
  and look with my own eyes at his Temple.
During danger he will keep me safe in his shelter.
  He will hide me in his Holy Tent,
  or he will keep me safe on a high mountain.
My head is higher than my enemies around me.
I will offer joyful sacrifices in his Holy Tent.
  I will sing and praise the LORD.

LORD, hear me when I call;
  have mercy and answer me.
My heart said of you, "Go, worship him."
  So I come to worship you, LORD.

I truly believe
  I will live to see the LORD's goodness.
Wait for the LORD's help.
  Be strong and brave,
  and wait for the LORD's help.
                          —*Psalm 27:1-8, 13-14*

YOUR RESPONSE

1. When the psalmist wanted help, he praised God. Why do you think he did this?

2. How can you worship the Lord while waiting for help?

Day 21

SOMEBODY'S RIGHT BEHIND YOU

Advice is good, but it can't replace the voice of God, telling us which way to turn.

ou've got to take this job. It's everything you've wanted!" My friend's voice grew louder, more insistent on the phone.

"Maybe," I sighed. "I just don't know . . ."

"Well, I think you're making a big mistake if you pass this up," he warned.

"I'm not so sure," I repeated, resenting his pushiness.

Equally frustrated with each other, we abruptly ended the conversation. I cradled the phone receiver and dropped to the couch in a heap of tears.

Recently I'd been offered a new job that would change my location, my entire life. Unfortunately, I couldn't decide whether to accept or reject it, and the stress was clobbering me.

What's wrong with me? I wondered. *I'm trying to make this decision the right way, but this is a disaster!*

For me, making a decision "the right way" included seeking counsel from Christians. In Proverbs 15:22, I'd read that "Plans fail without good advice, but they succeed with the advice of many others." So I solicited advice. I asked each person, "Do you

96

think I should take this new job?" But with each answer, I sank deeper into confusion, and I blamed God for not responding clearly.

Everyone I talked to seemed eager to help. Everyone meant well. But each adviser expressed a different opinion—and the conflicting advice muddled my thinking and paralyzed my decision making. I needed advice on sorting out the advice!

*Y*ou'd think such confusion would have stopped me. But no, I let fear propel me toward more advice. My current job had been difficult, and I didn't want to leap from the proverbial frying pan into the fire. So I panicked and talked to more friends, family, co-workers and just about anyone else who'd listen.

I might as well have worn a sign that read, "Anybody who wants to give advice, please talk to me." The results were just as devastating. I discovered that knowing people didn't qualify them as advisers. Some people felt uncomfortable giving advice while others spouted impulsive answers. Neither of these scenarios helped me, and the pressure mounted.

Unfortunately, my counselors weren't the problem. Because I didn't wisely choose advisers and carefully evaluate their advice, I rapidly destroyed myself. I resented my inability to decide and privately blamed everyone else for the standstill.

But far worse, I substituted people's opinions for spending time with God, reading the Scriptures, and asking Him for wisdom and strength. I was so busy running from person to person, I couldn't hear the quiet, steady voice right behind me. A voice that, all along, wanted to fulfill my desires and direct me in the right way.

Eventually, a deadline forced me to decide. I turned down that perfect-looking job. And for months I thought I'd made the wrong decision. But with hindsight, I realized my internal confusion had been God saying, "Wait. It's not time yet." If I'd listened to Him in the first place, I'd have saved myself much worry and panic. I'd felt as though God had overlooked my expectations when, in fact, I'd been ignoring Him!

Hopefully, when the next fear-provoking decision appears, I'll remember that, while advice is necessary and advantageous, it can't substitute for hearing from the God who stands right behind me.

❦

PERSONAL CHECKPOINT

1. How can you learn to hear God's voice?

2. Does pressure or disappointment block your ability to hear His voice? If so, how can you unstop the blockage?

GOD'S VIEWPOINT

A plea for God's help:

> God, hear my cry;
>> listen to my prayer.
> I call to you from the ends of the earth when I am afraid.
>> Carry me away to a high mountain.
> You have been my protection,
>> like a strong tower against my enemies.
>
> Let me live in your Holy Tent forever.
>> Let me find safety in the shelter of your wings.
> God, you have heard my promises.
>> You have given me what belongs to those who fear you.
>
> Give the king a long life;
>> let him live many years.
> Let him rule in the presence of God forever.
>> Protect him with your love and truth.
> Then I will praise your name forever,
>> and every day I will keep my promises.
>> —Psalm 61

Reassurance to God's people:

> This is what the Lord GOD, the Holy One of Israel, says:
>> "If you come back to me and trust me, you will be saved.
> If you will be calm and trust me, you will be strong."

The LORD wants to show his mercy to you.
He wants to rise and comfort you.
The LORD is a fair God,
and everyone who waits for his help will be happy.

You people who live on Mt. Zion in Jerusalem will not cry anymore. The LORD will hear your crying, and he will comfort you. When he hears you, he will help you. The LORD has given you sorrow and hurt like the bread and water you ate every day. He is your teacher; he will not continue to hide from you, but you will see your teacher with your own eyes. If you go the wrong way—to the right or to the left—you will hear a voice behind you saying, "This is the right way. You should go this way."
                                    —Isaiah 30:15, 18-21

YOUR RESPONSE

1. When you feel afraid, is it difficult to believe that God hears your prayers? Why, or why not?

2. How can you allow God to be your teacher?

WHAT ARE YOU DOING TODAY?

**We can reach tomorrow's dreams
by pursuing what needs to be done today.**

ased on the excitement of her creative writing class-rooms of the 1920s, Dorothea Brande wrote the book *Becoming a Writer* to teach young people the practical as well as the ethereal aspects of writing.

"If you are going in for a lifetime of writing," she wrote, "bursts of work are not what you are out to establish as your habit, but a good, steady, satisfying flow, rising occasionally to an extra-ordinary level of performance, but seldom falling below what you have discovered is your own normal output.

"A completely honest inventory, taken every two or three months, or twice a year at the least, will keep you up to the best and most abundant writing of which you are capable." [25]

Dorothea encouraged her students to accomplish some-thing each day toward their goal of writing.

Her admonition reminds me of a time when, as an author wannabe, I elaborately conversed with friends about my desire to write.

One of them, a disciplined musician, asked, "How much do you write every day?"

"Well, I don't write every day," I replied.

He looked surprised, but persisted.

"Then do you write on a regular basis?"

"Uh, no," I gulped.

"How can you become a writer if you don't write every day—or at least regularly?"

"Well, I guess I can't," I conceded.

I got the point. Until then, I'd been all talk and no action. It was time to write—or to find another dream.

Sometimes, when we look toward the future, we forget to accomplish what needs to be done today. About then, we could benefit from one of Dorothea's "honest inventories" about our progress. It begins with asking, "What am I doing today to accomplish my dreams for tomorrow?"

"Am I preparing for what's ahead?"

"Am I praying, asking for God's guidance?"

"Am I doing what I can accomplish, even if it's a small task?"

Usually, when we're waiting for something in the future, there's a piece of it we can accomplish today. Looking for tomorrow isn't an excuse for overlooking today. Like the recent campaign for running shoes, sometimes we need to "Just Do It."

PERSONAL CHECKPOINT

1. What can you do today to accomplish tomorrow's dreams?

2. Do you view the spiritual disciplines (prayer, Scripture reading, meditation, etc.) as part of accomplishing this goal? Why, or why not?

GOD'S VIEWPOINT

Jesus instructed His followers:

Don't store treasures for yourselves here on earth where moths and rust will destroy them and thieves can break in and steal them. But store your trea-

sures in heaven where they cannot be destroyed by moths or rust and where thieves cannot break in and steal them. Your heart will be where your treasure is.

The eye is a light for the body. If your eyes are good, your whole body will be full of light. But if your eyes are evil, your whole body will be full of darkness. And if the only light you have is really darkness, then you have the worst darkness.

No one can serve two masters. The person will hate one master and love the other, or will follow one master and refuse to follow the other. You cannot serve both God and worldly riches.

So I tell you, don't worry about the food or drink you need to live, or about the clothes you need for your body. Life is more than food, and the body is more than clothes. Look at the birds in the air. They don't plant or harvest or store food in barns, but your heavenly Father feeds them. And you know that you are worth much more than the birds. You cannot add any time to your life by worrying about it.

And why do you worry about clothes? Look at how the lilies in the field grow. They don't work or make clothes for themselves. But I tell you that even Solomon with his riches was not dressed as beautifully as one of these flowers. God clothes the grass in the field, which is alive today but tomorrow is thrown into the fire. So you can be even more sure that God will clothe you. Don't have so little faith! Don't worry and say, 'What will we eat?' or 'What will we drink?' or 'What will we wear?' The people who don't know God keep trying to get these things, and your Father in heaven knows you need them. The thing you should want most is God's kingdom and doing what God wants. Then all these other things you need will be given to you. So don't worry about tomorrow, because tomorrow will have its own worries. Each day has enough trouble of its own.

—*Matthew 6:19-34*

YOUR RESPONSE

1. How can you not worry about tomorrow, but still hope and work toward future dreams?

2. What keeps you from accomplishing today's necessities?

DON'T MISS THE GOOD STUFF

When we focus on what we don't have,
we can miss God's gifts to us.

henever I grow too focused on the problem at hand, I remind myself of a movie I saw last Easter with a couple of friends. After stuffing ourselves with quiche and dishing out ideas about what's wrong with life, we settled in the living room to let a videotape entertain us.

For the movie *Babette's Feast,* set in the late 1800s, filmmakers fleshed out Isak Dinesen's tale about a pious congregation on the desolate coast of Denmark. In this story, two elderly, unmarried sisters took in a French woman who had fled her country's unrest. Babette became the sisters' cook and housekeeper, preparing the codfish and ale-bread soup they requested each day.

For fourteen years, the three women existed together, permitting themselves not much more than church activities and knitting. But life momentarily changed when Babette won the French lottery. She decided to spend her winnings on a sumptuous feast for some townsfolk who squabbled among themselves.

Babette wanted to offer a peace meal to her neighbors, but they thought she'd gone mad, and they denounced her cooking as sin. Before the dinner, they covenanted to say nothing about the food.

Babette prepared the multi-course feast—a celebration of artistic cooking—and the townspeople, though they obviously enjoyed the food, never commented on it. They also failed to realize this dinner's effect on them: It melted the bitterness that had characterized their relationships for years.

When the guests left, Babette revealed to her employers that she once worked as the master chef at the finest restaurant in Paris. Yet, other than the two sisters, the townspeople expressed no regard for Babette's gift.

What narrowly focused people, I thought while watching the movie. But as the credits rolled, it hit me. In much the same way, I'd been overlooking God's good gifts to me.

I am an obsessive thinker. And passing through stress-filled days, I often blow out of proportion an immediate problem and eclipse the good around me.

A warm letter from a friend. A compliment from my boss. An unexpected refund. A comforting Scripture. These arrive as God's good gifts to me. But they usually get overlooked while I'm focusing on what feels like—at least to me—insurmountable trouble. Always, it's trouble that God hasn't solved yet. Often, I complain about His delayed response. But really, my myopic vision isn't fair to Him.

If I lift my eyes off the problem, I can spot God's gifts all around me. They may not be the answer I'm searching for at the moment, but they're good and continuous gifts that say, "I still love you, My child." They remind me that God doesn't stop caring for me, even though I live with unfulfilled expectations.

Now during the hard times, I remind myself to hunt for God's small surprises while I'm waiting for His big solution. It takes my mind off the problem. It helps me to trust Him. It deters me from the sin of ingratitude. It encourages me to know that God still cares.

I don't know about you, but in times of trouble, I need all of the encouragement I can get. And since trouble will always be part of this life, I can't afford to miss the good stuff.

❦

PERSONAL CHECKPOINT

1. What expectations keep you from recognizing God's good gifts?

2. How could you prompt yourself to notice these gifts?

GOD'S VIEWPOINT

The psalmist laments to God:

> *Sin speaks to the wicked in their hearts.*
> *They have no fear of God.*
> *They think too much of themselves*
> *so they don't see their sin and hate it.*
> *Their words are wicked lies;*
> *they are no longer wise or good.*
> *At night they make evil plans;*
> *what they do leads to nothing good.*
> *They don't refuse things that are evil.*
>
> *LORD, your love reaches to the heavens,*
> *your loyalty to the skies.*
> *Your goodness is as high as the mountains.*
> *Your justice is as deep as the great ocean.*
> *LORD, you protect both people and animals.*
> *God, your love is so precious!*
> *You protect people in the shadow of your wings.*
> *They eat rich food in your house,*
> *and you let them drink from your river of pleasure.*
> *You are the giver of life.*
> *Your light lets us enjoy life.*
>
> *Continue to love those who know you*
> *and to do good to those who are good.*

Don't let proud people attack me
and the wicked force me away.
Those who do evil have been defeated.
They are overwhelmed;
they cannot do evil any longer.
— *Psalm 36*

James reminds Christians:

Every good action and every perfect gift is from God. These good gifts come down from the Creator of the sun, moon, and stars, who does not change like their shifting shadows.
— *James 1:17*

FOR RESPONSE

1. What causes you to overlook your sin?

2. Will God give good gifts to you only if you're sinless? Why, or why not?

FORGET ABOUT
FORGETFULNESS

**God doesn't suffer memory lapses about
our desires. He remembers what matters to us.**

R ecently my mother told me a funny story about meeting up with her old friend Edna. In high school, she and Edna were inseparable, sharing the typical school-girl gossip, giggles, and outings.

"We were the best of friends," my mother explained, "and thought we always would be." But as often happens, the friendship fell away to marriage, children, and living miles apart from each other.

Then, two years ago at my uncle's funeral in their tiny hometown, Edna and Mom met again. It had been fifty years since high school, but they remembered the special relationship forged back then, and promised to get together.

A few months later, Edna visited my mother's town. Both women anticipated their reunion, expecting to recall the good times and to catch up on high school classmates.

"You won't believe what happened," my mother said, and described exchanges like this:

Mom: "Do you remember the time we skipped school?"

Edna: "Uh, no. When?" . . . "Whatever happened to Tom and Louise?"

Mom: "Tom and Louise? I don't remember them."

The women remembered they'd been friends, but couldn't recall the same events or people from their days together.

Mom handled the memory loss with her usual good humor. Laughing, she told me, "Don't lose your friends, Judy. When you're old, your brain can't find them again!"

*A*ctually, stories like this aren't new to me. For years, my family has majored on absentmindedness. It's especially accentuated at family gatherings:

"Please pass me the thingamajig over there."

"Now where did I put my keys?"

"What's-her-name called me the other day."

"Okay, who put the salt in the refrigerator?"

Nobody seems to care because we all understand each other. In a silly way, we wear it as our red badge of courage. I like to think of it as a family crest: to be Couchman is to be slightly adrift.

I particularly don't mind because there's a creative streak in my family, too. And often a preoccupied mind accompanies the creative soul. Besides, my mother sometimes forgets names and events, but she always remembers what matters to her children.

But believe me, I wouldn't want my family in charge of spinning the universe. And I find comfort in knowing the God who does. He assures me, "I will not forget you." He formed me in my mother's womb. He calls me by name. He counts the hairs on my head. He remembers my needs. He knows the plans He holds for me. He numbers my days. He doesn't forget my heart's desires, even though I'm still waiting for their fulfillment.

So while I love my family because it forgets little things, I cherish my heavenly Father because He remembers them. Passing through sunless days, I know He doesn't lose sight of me or where I'm going. He never forgets what matters to His children.

PERSONAL CHECKPOINT

1. What makes you feel as if the Lord has forgotten you?

2. When you feel this way, what could help you remember that God never forgets what matters to you?

GOD'S VIEWPOINT

A conversation between Isaiah and God:

> *Before I was born, the LORD called me to serve him.*
> *The LORD named me while I was still in my mother's body.*
> *He made my tongue like a sharp sword.*
> *He hid me in the shadow of his hand.*
> *He made me like a sharp arrow.*
> *He hid me in the holder for his arrows.*
> *He told me, "Israel, you are my servant.*
> *I will show my glory through you."*
> *But I said, "I have worked hard for nothing;*
> *I have used all my power, but I did nothing useful.*
> *But the LORD will decide what my work is worth;*
> *God will decide my reward."*
> *The LORD made me in the body of my mother*
> *to be his servant,*
> *to lead the people of Jacob back to him*
> *so that Israel might be gathered to him.*
> *The LORD will honor me,*
> *and I will get my strength from my God.*
>
> *This is what the LORD says:*
> *"At the right time I will hear your prayers.*
> *On the day of salvation I will help you."*

Heavens and earth, be happy.
   Mountains, shout with joy,
because the Lord comforts his people
   and will have pity on those who suffer.

But Jerusalem said, "The Lord has left me;
   the Lord has forgotten me."

The Lord answers, "Can a woman forget the baby she nurses?
   Can she feel no kindness for the child to which she gave birth?
Even if she could forget her children,
   I will not forget you.
See, I have written your name on my hand."
                                        —*Isaiah 49:1c-5, 8a-b, 13-16a*

Your Response

1. God says, "At the right time, I will hear your prayers." What might He mean by "the right time"?

2. How could you begin to accept God's comfort?

Part Five

YOUR DAY WILL COME

God won't keep you waiting forever

isappointments are often direct gateways to prosperity
in the very things we have thought they were going to
ruin forever. God's thwartings are often our grandest opportu-
nities. We start on a pathway that we think is going to lead us
to a desired end, but God in His providence thwarts us, and
then we rashly conclude that all is over, and are in despair.
But after a little while we find that that very thwarting has
been the divine opportunity for the success we desired; or, if
not for just that, for a far better thing that we would infinitely
rather have. He changes the very thing we thought was our
sorrow into our crown of joy. [26]

Hannah Whitall Smith,
The Common Sense Teaching of the Bible

*W*ithout a doubt, yesterday marked my favorite day of the year. It was May 15, the day gardeners in Colorado begin planting without the fear of frost. (Well, *almost* no fear.) The day we create masterpieces from our lowly plots of earth.

As an adult, not even Christmas, Thanksgiving, or my birthday has sparked such anticipation and delight within me. This morning, a Saturday, I leaped out of bed and almost hyperventilated over the creative possibilities. And while driving home after my third trip to a nursery, I felt myself grinning for no reason.

Well, maybe there was a reason.

Planting the flower beds means winter has passed and I can finally fulfill my dreams. Instead of fighting the cold, I'll soon be reveling in the beauty I'd imagined through darker days. I'm free to express the desires deep within me.

Still, it's more than flowers that captivate my heart these days. I'm also reminded that, in the seasons and in our lives, God never lets the darkness last forever.

A few days ago, I called a friend to tell her I'd accepted a job transfer within my organization. Absolutely, this position fulfills my desires in a way I'd never thought possible.

"You know, it wasn't until I'd given up my expectations that God surprised me with a job uniquely designed for me," I told her. "But it's not just the job. Writing books, living in a Victorian house—those were dreams, too, and God has answered them all within the same year!"

"How like God," she said, and we reminisced about the long years of dark disappointment that suddenly and unexpectedly have passed.

Yes, how like God. Just when we think there's no hope, He rushes in with a bundle of blessings. Who knows why? I sure don't. But I can use my story to encourage others who still wait for God's answers.

If anyone had given up on God's kindness, it was me. Outwardly, I played the role of the committed Christian, but inwardly, I'd stepped beyond merely surrendering my expectations. I'd shut down spiritually. My devotional life died; I succumbed to sin; my outlook grew cold and pessimistic. Secretly, I believed God loved everyone else but me; I believed that He'd answer their pleas, but never mine.

And despite it all, God swept in with love, grace, and the fulfillment of my desires.

I'm not advocating that when we're discouraged, we quit following the Scriptures and live however we please. But it's comforting to know that God's grace and power loom larger than any obstacle we face—and that His light shines brighter and penetrates deeper than our darkest despair.

The Apostle Paul said it's the kindness of God that leads us to repentance (Romans 2:4). We can depend on this kindness to redeem us from ourselves while we're waiting for His answers. And to assure us that, whether it's on earth or not until we reach heaven, God won't keep His children waiting forever.

PERSONAL CHECKPOINT

Part Five can help you keep hoping for the future and believing in God's good plans for you.

1. Do you still hope that God will fulfill your desires? Why, or why not?

2. What has been your inward response to God's delay of your desires? How do you feel about this response?

3. How can you draw encouragement from the stories of others who've received their desires?

TIMING IS EVERYTHING

The fulfillment of our desires depends on God's timetable.

Y ou couldn't argue with Gracie's logic," wrote her husband, comedian George Burns. "Sometimes you couldn't understand it, but you certainly couldn't argue with it." [27] One of his and Gracie Allen's comedy routines included this gem:

George: Gracie, how many days are there in a year?

Gracie: Seven.

George: Seven?

Gracie: Seven. Monday, Tuesday, Wednesday, Thursday, Friday, Saturday, and Sunday. If you know any more, George, just name them.

Evidently, Gracie's logic ran in her family. On Eddie Cantor's radio show, she explained:

Gracie: My brother has this wonderful idea for coffee that he invented. A spoonless spoon.

Eddie: A spoonless spoon?

Gracie: That's right. It's a spoon made of sugar. You can just put it in the cup of coffee.

Eddie: That's silly. You put it in the coffee and it goes to the bottom of the cup and then what happens?

Gracie: (Acting as though Cantor was dense.) Well, then, you take a regular spoon and you mix it up. [28]

George was right. Gracie's logic didn't make sense, but it's what made her delightful. For several decades, Burns and Allen entertained audiences with their unique humor. With George as the straight man and Gracie as the dizzy but lovable wife, they moved from vaudeville to radio to television—and into the hearts of millions.

For this husband and wife comedy team, everything depended on depending on each other. His questions set up her rapid-fire explanations. Her concluding one-liners needed his deadpan responses. The ability to reply at the right time—and in the appropriate manner—made their comedy sparkle.

It all depended on timing.

*T*here's a mystique about timing. When it's right, it's fabulous. When it's wrong, it's a disaster. It takes listening to the inner self to make it work. Not just in comedy, but in all of life.

We speak of the right timing to get married, to start a business, to have children, to change jobs, to risk a new venture, even to take a vacation. Some of us sense this timing intuitively; others plan it. Either way, we know that timing makes a difference. It affects our outlook and success, so sometimes we stop and say, "It's not the right time yet." And even if they don't understand, people make room for a delayed decision.

Oddly, we forget to give the same room to God.

Maybe it's because we know He's capable of doing anything, but we get impatient waiting for God. We forget that He waits for the right timing, too. In fact, He knows the *perfect* timing, even though it looks illogical to us. His ways are not our ways, and neither are His timetables our timetables.

But when we wait for His timing, nothing can compare with its abiding impact on us.

❀

PERSONAL CHECKPOINT

1. In your life right now, whose timetable are you following?

2. How might timing affect the fulfillment of your desires?

GOD'S VIEWPOINT

A teacher reflects on the seasons of life:

> *There is a time for everything,*
> *and everything on earth has its special season.*
> *There is a time to be born*
> *and a time to die.*
> *There is a time to plant*
> *and a time to pull up plants.*
> *There is a time to kill*
> *and a time to heal.*
> *There is a time to destroy*
> *and a time to build.*
> *There is a time to cry*
> *and a time to laugh.*
> *There is a time to be sad*
> *and a time to dance.*
> *There is a time to throw away stones*
> *and a time to gather them.*
> *There is a time to hug*
> *and a time not to hug.*
> *There is a time to look for something*
> *and a time to stop looking for it.*
> *There is a time to keep things*
> *and a time to throw things away.*
> *There is a time to tear apart*
> *and a time to sew together.*
> *There is a time to be silent*
> *and a time to speak.*
> *There is a time to love*
> *and a time to hate.*
> *There is a time for war*
> *and a time for peace.*

God has given them a desire to know the future. He does everything just right and on time, but people can never completely understand what he is doing. So I realize that the best thing for them is to be happy and enjoy themselves as long as they live. God wants all people to eat and drink and be happy in their work, which are gifts from God. I know that every-thing God does will continue forever. People cannot add anything to what God has done, and they cannot take anything away from it. God does it this way to make people respect him.

—Ecclesiastes 3:1-8, 11-14

YOUR RESPONSE

1. How can you learn to wait for and trust God's timing?

2. When you make decisions, how can you sense God's timing?

YOU GOTTA HAVE HOPE

Hope can help us hang on when the future looks bleak and out of control.

hen Marie entered the hospice, she didn't intend to die. The frail, fifty-three-year-old cancer victim said she'd leave not in a wheelchair or a body bag, but with her own strength. Quite a statement for someone who'd been depleted by radiation and the spread of cancer throughout her body.

Two days later, Marie's heart began giving out. A few days after that, she slipped into apnea, a forerunner to death. Her breathing grew slow and labored. No one expected her to last through the night.

Marie, however, had other things in mind. From somewhere deep inside her, she fought back. The medical team watched in disbelief as her breathing grew steadily stronger, her vital signs stabilized and her blood pressure reached 110/80. They quietly cheered her along, knowing she would not give up on life.

For several weeks after this incident, Marie got out of bed every day and walked a few steps. But then the doctors discovered cancer in her pancreas, and even high doses of morphine couldn't control the pain. They told Marie she'd be gambling to accept surgery, but she considered the options and signed the release forms. She hoped that surgery would relieve the pain and add to her life.

After the three-hour operation, Marie showed no sign of remission, but her bodily functions returned to normal. She began feeling stronger and walking without pain. She considered a hospital gown a sign of weakness, so she wore street clothes and asked, "When can I go home?"

The day Marie left the hospice, the halls lined with nurses and patients who watched her walk toward the door in a bright red dress, head held high. Someone clapped; then everyone joined in.

Marie had hoped, and she survived. [29]

*W*hen life pushes against us, we need hope to fight back. People like Marie remind us that, although hope isn't tangible, we can observe it thriving in the human spirit. It is God's gift to keep us breathing, moving, battling for our lives when we're pressed by confusion or adversity or disappointment.

Hope thrives best in the hard times. The Bible says, "We also exult in our tribulations, knowing that tribulation brings about perseverance; and perseverance, proven character; and proven character, hope; and hope does not disappoint, because the love of God has been poured out within our hearts through the Holy Spirit who was given to us" (Romans 5:3-5; NASV).

Yet hope isn't something we can conjure up as needed. It's the outflow of God's love in our hearts. And if we're without hope, we can ask Him to renew it, just as He revitalizes the Holy Spirit's work within us. Without hope, people perish. With God's hope, they believe beyond themselves.

For example, Opal's doctor told her not to get pregnant again. Instead, she needed a hysterectomy. But for reasons beyond her understanding, Opal risked another pregnancy that landed her in bed for several months so she wouldn't lose the baby.

Opal had hope.

Despite these efforts, the baby entered life—and an incubator—two months ahead of her delivery date. The tiny daughter weighed less than four pounds and, every day after her discharge from the hospital, Opal checked on the baby's progress.

"It was awful, always feeling afraid that she wouldn't survive," said Opal. "But I kept hoping and praying that God would let her live." A month later, she brought home a healthy baby.

"Somehow, I knew that God wanted me to have my baby. That he had something for her to do," she added.

I believe that, despite all odds, God places hope in our hearts for a reason. And if we cling to it, we'll survive to reap a priceless "proven character" and probably our unfulfilled desires.

Why do I believe the odds fall in our favor?

I am Opal's daughter.

PERSONAL CHECKPOINT

1. What is your definition of hope?

2. Is hope alive in your life? Why, or why not?

GOD'S VIEWPOINT

Praise to the God of hope:

Praise be to the God and Father of our Lord Jesus Christ. In God's great mercy he has caused us to be born again into a living hope, because Jesus Christ rose from the dead. Now we hope for the blessings God has for his children. These blessings, which cannot be destroyed or be spoiled or lose their beauty, are kept in heaven for you. God's power protects you through your faith until salvation is shown to you at the end of time. This makes you very happy, even though now for a short time different kinds of troubles may make you sad. These troubles come to prove that your faith is pure. This purity of faith is worth more than gold, which can be proved to be pure by fire but will ruin. But the purity of your faith will bring you praise and glory and honor when Jesus Christ is shown to you. You have not seen Christ, but still you love him. You cannot see him now, but you believe in him. So you are filled with a joy that cannot be explained, a joy full of glory. And you are receiving the goal of your faith—the salvation of your souls.

The prophets searched carefully and tried to learn about this salvation. They prophesied about the grace that was coming to you. The Spirit of Christ was in the prophets, telling in advance about the sufferings of Christ and about the glory that would follow those sufferings. The prophets tried to learn about what the Spirit was showing them, when those things would happen, and what the world would be like at that time. It was shown them that their service was not for themselves but for you, when they told about the truths you have now heard. Those who preached the Good News to you told you those things with the help of the Holy Spirit who was sent from heaven—things into which angels desire to look.

So prepare your minds for service and have self-control. All your hope should be for the gift of grace that will be yours when Jesus Christ is shown to you. Now that you are obedient children of God do not live as you did in the past. You did not understand, so you did the evil things you wanted. But be holy in all you do, just as God, the One who called you, is holy. It is written in the Scriptures: "You must be holy, because I am holy."

You were bought, not with something that ruins like gold or silver, but with the precious blood of Christ, who was like a pure and perfect lamb. Christ was chosen before the world was made, but he was shown to the world in these last times for your sake.

—1 Peter 1:3-16, 18c-20

YOUR RESPONSE

1. How might you increase your hope?

2. How can you know if your hope is placed in God or in yourself?

MIRACLES STILL HAPPEN

***God still performs supernatural feats,
even when we forget to ask for them.***

*I*f ever I'd felt cornered, this was the moment.

"We already have a cat. We can't take another one in our condo," said Debbie, who lived across the porch from me.

"I have a cat, a dog, and two birds," chimed in Babs, my friend downstairs. "So could you take this cat in? Just for the night?"

The feline in question was a chubby tabby who'd spent a few evenings meowing around our doorsteps. Nobody paid much attention to her at first. But the weather had turned bitter cold and she seemed hungry.

"But I hate cats," I protested. "I mean, I really hate them!"

Their eyes pleaded.

I sighed, hoping they'd relent.

They didn't.

"Okay, you guys, but just for tonight," I heard myself say. And thanks to my neighbors, I lugged a Garfield look-alike, some canned cat food, and a bag of kitty litter up to my place a few minutes later.

"After all, tomorrow is Thanksgiving," I mumbled as I picked off the fur on my coat. "But I'll never change," I told the cat and dropped her food in a dish. "I really hate cats."

I hated them so much that when I visited friends I'd barely sit in the same room with their cats. I loved the humorous books about "what to do with a dead cat," but wouldn't think of buying a card or anything else with the likeness of a feline on it. I didn't want anyone to think I even remotely liked those snobby animals.

So that night, lying in the dark, listening for animal noises, I never suspected the transformation to come. I didn't want a pet. I didn't like the responsibility. And I definitely hated cats.

I can't recall the exact turning point. Maybe it was when, one morning a few days later, she jumped on the bed and nuzzled my arm. Or when she discreetly and neatly used the kitty litter. (Very impressive. Growing up, my family got up in the night to let the dog out.) Or when a stranger answered my lost-and-found ad, and I suddenly hoped this cat wasn't hers.

Whatever it was, within a few days I fell irrevocably in love with this bumpkin of a cat. So much so, that one of my friends finally believes in miracles. And almost five years later, others still stifle laughter when they watch me dote on Mercedes.

But I don't care. I really love my cat.

So much so, that I'm clipping coupons for gourmet pet food, nauseating people with cute cat stories, fending off enemies like neighborhood dogs and fur-grabbing kids, plopping her into my bed at night, and wondering how I'll survive when she dies.

Mercedes arrived at my home during a difficult time, and she unexpectedly uncorked the tenderness I'd stuffed inside of me. She's helped quell loneliness. She's taught me that I'm not too selfish or too busy or too inflexible to really care—about small animals, needy people, or whomever God sends into my future. But most of all, she's taught me that miracles still happen.

To write about miracles, I could have described how, as a young child, He healed me from asthma. Or how, as a young adult, He spared me from an excruciating death by malignant melanoma. These were miracles. Yet the miracle of Mercedes touches me the most of all.

Mercedes reminds me that God isn't too busy performing extravagant feats to care about the small, everyday kind of stuff. He's the God of the small, medium, large, and everything-in-between miracles. He tailors His supernatural performance to exactly what we need—even when we don't know we need it.

When I stroke Mercedes, I remember that, with God, all things are possible. Sinners become saints. Old habits melt into new virtues. Cat haters turn into cat lovers. Hard-to-imagine dreams come true. Often it happens when it's least expected, in ways I'd never imagine.

Looking ahead, the miracle of Mercedes helps me to believe that God can still breathe into existence my other unfulfilled desires. In the meantime, I can enjoy His love and attention—and a cuddly, gentle cat—while I'm waiting.

I believe that for you, too. Well, minus the cat if you don't like felines. But I warn you, miracles still happen!

PERSONAL CHECKPOINT

1. Do you believe that God still performs miracles?

2. Is there a miracle you'd like to hope for, but it seems too impossible?

GOD'S VIEWPOINT

Praise for the God of miracles:

> *I will always sing about the LORD's love;*
> *I will tell of his loyalty from now on.*
> *I will say, "Your love continues forever;*
> *your loyalty goes on and on like the sky."*
> *You said, "I made an agreement with the man of my choice;*
> *I made a promise to my servant David.*
> *I told him, 'I will make your family continue forever.*
> *Your kingdom will go on and on.'"*
>
> *LORD, the heavens praise you for your miracles*
> *and for your loyalty in the meeting of your holy ones.*
> *Who in heaven is equal to the LORD?*
> *None of the angels is like the LORD.*
> *When the holy ones meet, it is God they fear.*

He is more frightening than all who surround him.
Lord GOD All-Powerful, who is like you?
  LORD, you are powerful and completely trustworthy.
You rule the mighty sea
  and calm the stormy waves.
You crushed the sea monster Rahab;
  by your power you scattered your enemies.

The skies and the earth belong to you.
  You made the world and everything in it.
You created the north and the south.
  Mount Tabor and Mount Hermon sing for joy at your name.
Your arm has great power.
  Your hand is strong; your right hand is lifted up.
Your kingdom is built on what is right and fair.
  Love and truth are in all you do.

Happy are the people who know how to praise you.
  LORD, let them live in the light of your presence.
In your name they rejoice
  and continually praise your goodness.
You are their glorious strength,
  and in your kindness you honor our king.
Our king, our shield, belongs to the LORD,
  to the Holy One of Israel.
                              —*Psalm 89:1-18*

YOUR RESPONSE

1. What keeps you from trusting God for a miracle?

2. How can you begin to believe Him for the seemingly impossible?

FEEL THE FEAR
AND DO IT

*We can allow fear to keep us from
our desires, or to propel us toward them.*

on't be afraid," said the Shepherd gently. "You are in my
service, and if you will trust me they will not be able to
force you against your will into any family alliance."

"I know, oh, I know," cried Much-Afraid, "but whenever I
meet any relatives I seem to lose all strength and simply cannot
resist them, no matter how hard I strive!" [30]

So begins the turmoil of Much-Afraid, the protagonist in
Hannah Hurnard's *Hind's Feet on High Places*. Should she follow
her Shepherd to the mountains? Or stay in the valley below with
her relatives? She knows either choice means difficulty.

If Much-Afraid follows the loving Shepherd, He will heal her
disfigured face and feet—and her even more crippling fear. But
first she must embark on a journey to the high places with travel-
ing companions called Sorrow and Suffering.

Though captivated by the Shepherd's love, Much-Afraid is
tempted to stay in the Valley of Humiliation. Not exactly an uplift-
ing community, but at least it's familiar. She worries about her
relatives, the Fearings. Maybe she could serve the Shepherd in her
neighborhood. Didn't these gloomy people need His love, too?

Besides, the relatives are pressuring her. When they uncovered her plan to leave, Much-Afraid's aunts, uncles, and cousins launched an all-out campaign to keep her home. Hadn't they taken her in as an orphan? Raised her as their own? What kind of gratitude was this? She should stay and marry a nice boy like Craven Fear, settle down and forget treacherous ideas like mountain climbing. Wasn't family important to her?

The Fearings' ravings pound in Much-Afraid's head as she tries to decide.

*L*ike Much-Afraid, we can feel frightened when confronted with the probability of fulfilling long-awaited desires. It's one thing to talk and pray about our dreams; it's quite another to embark on a journey to fulfill them! The enemy of our souls—even friends and family—can fuel our fear and, literally or figuratively, keep us "safe" at home.

Think about it, though. Which is really safer? Living with the loneliness and regret of giving into fear? Or, with God, launching out toward our dreams, despite the fear?

Dr. Lloyd Ogilvie, pastor and radio personality, wrote that "fear is really loneliness for God" and that we can claim His promise to never leave or forsake us. Only with God, can we find true safety and become "fearless and free" to pursue our great expectations. [31]

A recent book title coined a significant phrase for people holding themselves back from their desires: *Feel the Fear and Do It Anyway*. I like that. Even more, I need that. It shoves me away from the "safety" of waiting and into the adventure of living. Sometimes I rail at God for stalling, when He's not putting me on hold at all. Instead, I keep Him waiting by clinging to fear.

When we live with unfulfilled desires, it might be good to look around. We may find God right beside us, waiting for us to plunge past the fear, take His hand, and get on with it.

PERSONAL CHECKPOINT

1. What scares you about fulfilling your dreams?

2. How can you begin to believe that God will never forsake you, despite your fear?

GOD'S VIEWPOINT

Praise for God's help during fearful times:

> I love the LORD,
>> because he listens to my prayers for help.
> He paid attention to me,
>> so I will call to him for help as long as I live.
> The ropes of death bound me,
>> and the fear of the grave took hold of me.
> I was troubled and sad.
> Then I called out the name of the LORD.
>> I said, "Please, LORD, save me!"
>
> The LORD is kind and does what is right;
>> our God is merciful.
> The LORD watches over the foolish;
>> when I was helpless, he saved me.
> I said to myself, "Relax,
>> because the LORD takes care of you."
> LORD, you saved me from death.
>> You stopped my eyes from crying;
>> you kept me from being defeated.
> So I will walk with the LORD
>> in the land of the living.
> I believed, so I said,
>> "I am completely ruined."
> In my distress I said,
>> "All people are liars."
>
> What can I give the LORD
>> for all the good things he has given to me?
> I will lift up the cup of salvation,
>> and I will pray to the LORD.
> I will give the LORD what I promised
>> in front of all his people.

The death of one that belongs to the LORD
  is precious in his sight.
LORD, I am your servant;
  I am your servant and the son of your female servant.
  You have freed me from my chains.
I will give you an offering to show thanks to you,
  and I will pray to the LORD.
I will give the LORD what I promised
  in front of all his people,
in the Temple courtyards
  in Jerusalem.

Praise the LORD!

—Psalm 116

YOUR RESPONSE

1. What are the root causes of your fear? What can you do to face and fight fear?

2. How can you plunge past fear into your personal vision?

WHERE HE LEADS ME

Despite our unfulfilled desires,
God still holds good plans for us.

*I*n the novel *The Last Year of the War,* Jo attends Calvary Bible Institute—and she's got trouble. She's receiving unwanted and obnoxious attention from Clyde, a less-than-desirable classmate. In desperation, Jo discusses the problem with Miss Mackey, a school proctor:

> "Jo . . . how do you feel about Clyde McQuade? That is, do you feel, oh . . . scorn or pity, say?"
> "Both sometimes."
> "Both? . . . Disgust?"
> "Yes."
> "Can we say there has been no love?"
> "No love."
> "I mean, of course, Christian love."
> "Oh. No. Not much love. . . .To tell you the truth, I wouldn't care if I never saw him again in my life."
> Miss Mackey looked startled. Jo thought perhaps she was the first person to utter such words in this

office. She had meant it as a kind of confession. It came out like a curse.

"That's a heavy burden," Miss Mackey said. She stood and walked to the window, looking down into the street.

"Jo, what if you were to go to the mission field and find he is a fellow worker? Someone with whom you must work for years and years?"

"That would be very hard."

Miss Mackey turned. "How do you perceive your future with regard to Clyde, Jo?"

Future. Years stretched ahead with Clyde at her side. "I don't know. . . . I want to do the right thing . . . I mean now."

"What would Jesus do? Have you asked yourself that?"

"Jesus?" She said it as if she had never heard of Him before. "Oh, Jesus would—Isn't that different?"

"He would love him, wouldn't He?" Miss Mackey came back and sat on the edge of the desk. She cocked her head. "Are you *willing* to love Clyde, Jo?"

"Love him?" The word snagged her again.

"With Christ's love."

"I'm not sure what that would mean. It's very complicated."

"Are you willing to love him romantically?"

"Oh, no. Even Clyde himself hasn't—"

"I'm asking you about your own attitude, that's all. Are you willing to fall in love with him?"

"Oh, I couldn't."

"But God *could* make you love him. He could make Clyde attractive to you, if that was His plan. The question is, are you *willing* for that?" [32]

*P*oor Jo. If she follows God's leading, she could wind up married to a man she can't stand. At least that's what Miss Mackey thinks.

But Miss Mackey has a warped idea of the Spirit's leading and what it means to follow Him. She seems to feel that saying yes to God means resigning oneself to experiencing the worst that could possibly happen.

Unfortunately, many of us harbor a similar misunderstanding of God's ways. We're secretly afraid that if He doesn't fulfill our desires, God will guide us into distasteful—if not downright humiliating—situations. In other words, He'll ask us to do the very thing we don't want to do. We overemphasize sacrifice to the point of paralysis, and as a result, we're enthusiastic about following the Spirit's leading only when we're reasonably sure of the destination.

So what's the truth? Even though circumstances look dubious now, God says He has good plans for us, not plans to hurt us (Jeremiah 29:11) and He's sent the Holy Spirit to help us along the way. Instead of fearing torment, we can trust a God who wants what's best for us. [33]

It takes time, sometimes years. So we must wait and give up our doubts that God knows what He's doing. Because, eventually, God will fulfill our driving desires—or give us something better to replace them.

Either way, we win.

PERSONAL CHECKPOINT

1. How do you feel about following God's plan for you?

2. In the past, how has God proven that He has your best in mind?

GOD'S VIEWPOINT

Jeremiah comforts the captives in Babylon:

This is what the LORD says: "Babylon will be powerful for seventy years. After that time I will come to you, and I will keep my promise to bring you back to Jerusalem. I say this because I know what I am planning for you," says the Lord. "I have good plans for you, not plans to hurt you. I will give you hope and a good future. Then you will call my name. You will come to me and pray to me, and I will listen to you. You will search for me. And when you search for me with all your heart, you will find me! I will let you find me," says the LORD. "And I will bring you back from your captiv-

ity. I forced you to leave this place, but I will gather you from all the nations, from the places I have sent you as captives," says the LORD. "And I will bring you back to this place."

—Jeremiah 29:10-14

YOUR RESPONSE

1. Despite your circumstances, how can you continue to believe that God keeps your best in mind?

2. How can you learn to trust God's leading?

30

DIM REFLECTIONS ON LIFE

We won't fully understand God's ways until we meet Him face-to-face in heaven.

ue and I were neither close friends nor strangers in high school. She was a grade behind me, but since we both sang in the a cappella choir and I took voice lessons from her mother, we crossed paths repeatedly.

With our common interests, it would have been natural for us to chum around together. But I was a borderline brooder and Sue seemed the happy-go-lucky type. We kept a friendly but safe distance from each other.

Then in college, Sue and I bumped into each other at a Christian coffeehouse. She'd become a believer and, in my opinion, was thinking deeper thoughts. I'd learned it was okay to be a Christian and to enjoy life (although Sue never got me to very many parties). We became friends.

Sue and I talked a lot—at hamburger joints, after worship services, in our parents' homes. The more we interacted, the more we discovered how similar we really were. I soon learned that Sue wrestled with deep issues about herself, her faith, her family. But I didn't worry about it much; most of our generation struggled with "finding" themselves.

I wish I'd worried. Over the next few years, Sue's battles escalated into full-scale war. Eventually, she became severely depressed, retreating somewhere deep inside herself to escape anxiety. When she'd return with cries for help, no one could heal her. Not family, friends, doctors, or counselors. Even medication and shock treatments failed.

Desperate, Sue finally placed herself under the guardianship of a Christian ministry miles away from home. None of us cared for the organization, but we supported Sue's decision. We knew her alternative choice might be suicide. So for days, a ministry staff member read Scripture to Sue. Someone altered her diet. Others prayed—and God delivered her from despondency.

Rather than returning to our hometown, Sue got a job at the organization. She also sang in a quartet that accompanied the ministry's founder to speaking engagements around the country. He piloted them to each location in a small aircraft.

Once, the group visited our city, and I sat in the back row of a Baptist church, marveling at Sue's confident testimony and thanking God for still performing miracles. When I talked to her after the service, the Lord's presence felt unmistakable.

Several months later, the group's plane crashed while flying to a meeting. No one survived.

"How sad," said a friend, "that God took Sue when she was only twenty-eight years old. She never got to enjoy a full life and to see her dreams come true."

I've pondered my friend's lament since Sue's death. And though I don't understand why the Lord took Sue, I believe she lived a complete life. Once touched by God, she lived wholly for Him—and that's more than many of us accomplish in a three-score-and-ten lifetime.

B esides, we get so wrapped up in our own expectations that we forget God's timeline for us. He's ordained our days, and no amount of haggling will erase the eventuality that someday we'll discard our earth-bound bodies. Still, we can make a difference while passing through this world.

Someone once said that the best revenge is to live well. Our best revenge on sin and death is to live in the Holy Spirit's joy and love, despite our circumstances. If I had to choose, I'd rather live a short life filled with God's adventures and goodness than a long life of futility and despair. And if I knew my life would end soon, I'd want to fill those days with as much meaning and laughter as possible. I'd probably also realize how much time I'd wasted fretting about expectations that, in the light of eternity, really don't matter.

The Bible says that, for now, we can only see a dim reflection of God's workings in the world (1 Corinthians 13:12). Until we arrive in heaven, we won't fully understand why God fulfilled some of our desires and not others. Or why inequities exist among His dealings with people. As the sovereign Creator, these are His choices. But we can savor these days—or waste them away with rebellion.

He's left that up to us.

PERSONAL CHECKPOINT

1. What expectations would you like to fulfill before you die?

2. What expectations do you have no control over? Which ones could you do something about?

GOD'S VIEWPOINT

The most important aspect of life:

I may speak in different languages of people or even angels. But if I do not have love, I am only a noisy bell or a crashing cymbal. I may have the gift of prophecy. I may understand all the secret things of God and have all knowledge, and I may have faith so great I can move mountains. But even with all these things, if I do not have love, then I am nothing. I may give away everything I have, and I may even give my body as an offering to be burned. But I gain nothing if I do not have love.

Love is patient and kind. Love is not jealous, it does not brag, and it is not proud. Love is not rude, is not selfish, and does not get upset with others. Love does not count up wrongs that have been done. Love is not happy with evil but is happy with the truth. Love patiently accepts all things. It always trusts, always hopes, and always remains strong.

Love never ends. There are gifts of prophecy, but they will be ended. There are gifts of speaking in different languages, but those gifts will stop. There is the gift of knowledge, but it will come to an end. The reason is that our knowledge and our ability to prophesy are not perfect. But when perfection comes, the things that are not perfect will end. When I was a child, I talked like a child, I thought like a child, I reasoned like a child. When I became a man, I stopped those childish ways. It is the same with us. Now we see a dim reflection, as if we were looking into a mirror, but then we shall see clearly. Now I know only a part, but then I will know fully, as God has known me. So these three things continue forever: faith, hope, and love. And the greatest of these is love.

—1 Corinthians 13

YOUR RESPONSE

1. In light of eternity, what expectations could you release to God?

2. How could you bring more joy and meaning to your days, despite unmet expectations?

Notes

Part 1: Tall Tales

1. Cheryl Forbes, *Catching Sight of God* (Portland: Multnomah Press, 1987), p. 14. Used by permission.

2. G.B. Harrison, ed. *Shakespeare: The Complete Works* (New York: Harcourt, Brace & World, 1968), p. 1029.

3. Clifton Fadiman, gen. ed. *The Little, Brown Book of Anecdotes* (Boston: Little, Brown and Company, 1985), p. 367.

4. Fadiman, p. 440.

5. Ralph G. Martin, *Henry & Clare: An Intimate Portrait of the Luces* (New York: G.P. Putnam's Sons, 1991), p. 408.

6. Adaptation of "The Emperor's New Clothes" by Hans Christian Andersen. For the complete story, see *Hans Christian Andersen: The Complete Fairy Tales and Stories,* edited by Erik Christian Haugaard (New York: Doubleday, 1974), pp. 77-81.

Part 2: Caught in the Reality Gap

7. Alice Slaikeu Lawhead, *The Lie of the Good Life* (Portland: Multnomah Press, 1989), p. 16. Used by permission.

8. Janet Kobobel, *Where Is God When I Need Him Most?* (Colorado Springs: NavPress, 1991), p. 21.

9. Frank S. Mead, *The Encyclopedia of Religious Quotations* (Old Tappan: Fleming H. Revell , 1965), p. 1.

10. This reading first appeared in *If I'm So Good, Why Don't I Act That Way?* by Judith Couchman (Colorado Springs: NavPress, 1991), pp. 9–11, 20. Used by permission.

11. Paul Scott, *The Jewel in the Crown* (New York: Avon Books, 1979), p. 120.

12. John Bunyan, *The Pilgrim's Progress* (New York: Holt, Rinehart and Winston, 1961), p. 158.

13. Scott Elledge, *E.B. White* (New York: W. W. Norton & Company, 1984), p. 346.

14. Elledge, p. 346.

Part 3: WHY NOT ME, LORD?

15. Kobobel, p. 49. Used by permission.

16. John Bartlett, ed. *Bartlett's Familiar Quotations* (Boston: Little, Brown and Company, 1980), p. 781.

17. Judith Couchman, "At Least You Can Point Me Toward the Right Direction." *Christian Life*, October 1986, p. 6.

18. Colette Dowling, *Perfect Women* (New York: Avon Books, 1979), p. 43.

19. M. Scott Peck, *The Road Less Traveled* (New York: Simon & Schuster, 1978), p. 42.

20. Peck, p. 273.

21. Antoni Gronowicz, *Garbo: Her Story* (New York: Simon & Schuster, 1990), pp. 245, 249.

22. *Aesop's Fables* (New York: Grosset and Dunlap, 1947), pp. 52-54.

Part 4: Living in the Now

23. Amy Carmichael, *His thoughts said . . . His father said* (Fort Washington, PA: Christian Literature Crusade, nd), pp. 57–58. Used by permission.

24. Martha Graham, *Blood Memory* (New York: Doubleday, 1991), pp. 3-4.

25. Dorothea Brande, *Becoming a Writer* (Los Angeles: J.P. Tarcher, Inc., 1981), p. 96.

Part 5: Your Day Will Come

26. Hannah Whitall Smith, *The Common Sense Teaching of the Bible* (Old Tappan, NJ: Revell Publishers, 1985), p. 88. Used by permission.

27. George Burns, *Gracie: A Love Story* (New York: G.P. Putnam's Sons, 1988), p. 99.

28. Burns, pp. 95–96.

29. Robert Veninga, *The Gift of Hope* (Boston: Little, Brown and Company, 1985), pp. 11–13.

30. Hannah Hurnard, *Hind's Feet on High Places* (Wheaton: Tyndale House, 1984), p. 21.

31. Lloyd Ogilvie, *12 Steps to Living Without Fear* (Irving, Tex.: Word, 1987), pp. 11, 13.

32. Shirley Nelson, *The Last Year of the War* (San Francisco: Harper & Row, 1973), n.p.

33. Part of this reading first appeared in "Where He Leads Me, I Will Follow" by Judith Couchman from *Adult Creative Teaching Aids* (Elgin, IL: David C. Cook Publishing, n.d.) n.p. Used by permission.

For More Reading

Couchman, Judith. *Why Is Her Life Better Than Mine?* Colorado Springs: NavPress, 1991.

Cox, Alice Lawson. *Will the Pain Ever Go Away?* Colorado Springs: NavPress, 1991.

Kobobel, Janet. *Where Is God When I Need Him Most?* Colorado Springs: NavPress, 1991.

Lawhead, Alice Slaikeu. *The Lie of the Good Life.* Portland: Multnomah Press, 1989.

Ogilvie, Lloyd. *12 Steps to Living Without Fear.* Irving, Tex.: Word, 1987.

Peck, M. Scott. *The Road Less Traveled.* New York: Simon & Schuster, 1978.

Veniga, Robert. *A Gift of Hope: How We Survive Our Tragedies.* Boston: Little, Brown & Co., 1985.

Viorst, Judith. *Necessary Losses.* New York: Simon and Schuster, 1986.

Yancey, Philip. *Where Is God When It Hurts?* Grand Rapids: Zondervan Publishing House, 1977.

About the Author

Judith Couchman is Director of Product Development for the Periodicals Group of NavPress and a free-lance writer. Through her writing, she wants to "encourage people to find help and comfort in a loving and forgiving God."

Judith has published many times in magazines and curriculum publications and formerly worked as the editor of *Sunday Digest* and *Christian Life*. She's taught writing at conferences around the United States and has received honors from professional organizations for her work in secondary education, religious publishing, and corporate communications.

With this release, Judith has published five books. She holds a B.S. in education and an M.A. in journalism and putters in her flower gardens while procrastinating on deadlines. She lives in Colorado Springs, Colorado.